PRODUCTION MANAGEMENT

Joe Aveline

ENTERTAINMENT TECHNOLOGY PRESS

Application & Techniques Series

To the late Nat Brenner who knew a thing or two about
Production Management and Douglas Cornelissen
for whom the best is just about acceptable.

ENTERTAINMENT TECHNOLOGY PRESS

In taking advantage of the latest in 'print on demand' digital printing techniques, Entertainment Technology Press is approaching book publishing in a very different way. By establishing a wide range of highly specific technical books that can be kept up-to-date in a continuing publishing process, our plan is to cover the entertainment technology sector with a wide range of individual titles.

As will be seen by examining the back cover of this book, the ETP list is divided into various categories so as to allow sufficient room for generic growth and development of each title. To ensure the quality of the books and the success of the project the publishers are building up a team of authors who are practising in and well-respected by the industry. As specialists within a particular field of activity it is anticipated that each author will stay closely involved with 'their' title or titles for an extended period.

All Entertainment Technology Press titles have a dedicated area on the publisher's own website at www.etnow.com where latest information and up-dates can be accessed by purchasers of the books concerned. This additional service is included within the purchase price of all titles.

Readers and prospective authors are invited to submit any ideas and comments they may have on the Entertainment Technology Press series to the Series Editor either by post to the address below or by email to editor@etnow.com.

1 Kiln House Tel: +4

Ralph Koltai's design for the opening sequence of Back to Methuselah.

PRODUCTION MANAGEMENT

Joe Aveline

Entertainment Technology Press

Production Management
© Joe Aveline

First Published September 2002 by
Entertainment Technology Press Ltd
1 Kiln House Yard, Baldock Street, Royston, Hertfordshire SG8 5AY
Internet: www.etnow.com

ISBN 1 904031 10 2

A title within the
Entertainment Technology Press Application & Techniques Series
Series editor: John Offord

ACKNOWLEDGEMENTS

Thanks are due for all the help they have given during the
production of this book to:

Simon Corder
Ralph Koltai
John W. Jacobsen (White Oak Design)
Sue Mackinnon
the Entertainment Technology Press team

and photographs appear courtesy of:

The Merchant of Venice - Anthony Crickmay, V&A Picture Library
The White Devil - Zoe Dominic
Back to Methuselah - Ralph Koltai
Elizabethan Pageant - White Oak Design, Marblehead, Mass. USA

This book has no boundary except language. There is no telling where the reader might be while perusing this page. There is one crucial area of modern theatre work that is alluded to but not addressed in any great detail and that is safety. Safety in this context should be taken to include all the statutory and legal bases within which we work.

The reason is that there is within the UK alone ample evidence that regulations are not being applied with any degree of homogeneity throughout the land. We hear also of different ways of approaching such matters in other countries. Here too, in the UK, variations and changes are an almost constant diet. In this climate it did not seem appropriate to discuss something which could be obsolete by the time the ink is dry.

Nevertheless these are issues which the Production Manager must address. The only secure recommendation has to be to use the same principles as outlined in the book and assess the pecking order of the regulators and learn where to put the question. As with everything else, it will pay to keep abreast of current regulations and how they are being applied. Be confident in your approach.

And remember! There was a Safety conference in 1991. A speaker from the Home Office was taking questions and was asked what would be the best thing to do if you seriously disagreed with an inspector. Her reply was to challenge him - 'it might be his first day on the job!'

So, be proactive.

CONTENTS

Cut Your Coat According To Your Cloth

During my time at the Theatre Royal, E15, we always seemed to be 'up against it'. In some cases, the productions were simply rather large in concept. In others the powers that were did not programme far enough in advance and work on a new production often started late and we were always in hurry mode.

Then we did Ibsen's *Ghosts*. The designer produced an island setting of great simplicity except for a spider-like conservatory window through which the sun could rise at the end. Everything went very smoothly. So smoothly, that on the opening day the stage management and crew stood and sat around the set after the final dress rehearsal in a most relaxed and easy manner, all the work having been done. Not our normal last minute rush.

By chance, we had hit the golden mean. None of our resources, human or material, had been stretched – a super cast gave added pleasure to working on this production. It was a learning opportunity for me. I analysed all the factors – a small acting area better suited our limited stock of lighting and gave us greater possibilities of subtlety; a standing set meant clear wings and easy journeys – stage management well capable of propping, and wardrobe easily able to make the few dresses that were needed. Longer-term recollection and reconsideration led also to the realisation that this situation can only apply when all departments work within their scope. Any one department being put under stress will have a knock-on effect. It may interrupt the work-flow of others or, in extreme cases, involve others pitching in to help.

Later experiences have only served to reinforce the 'cut your cloth' syndrome. The real issue is to know where the various 'break-points' lie.

PROLOGUE

In 1988, when I was younger and even more foolish than I am now, I bit off more than I could chew. It was an open-air festival with several venues and hundreds of performances. I was the Technical Director, and my carefully constructed plans were dissolving even as I looked on. A few days before the festival opened it was becoming clear that the labyrinth of letters, schedules, and drawings I had sent around the world to my colleagues, while not obviously or necessarily flawed, had not all been consumed in exactly the spirit I had intended.

Exhaustion was setting in, I had woken in the back of a van that morning after two hours sleep. Judgement was fading. And then standing in the site-office was a funny looking old man, wearing big glasses and a fishing hat. My assistant had pulled a favour and Joe Aveline breezed in. "What can I do to help?" he asked.

I think he spent a fortnight with us, but I only really recall that first impression. We walked over to the big top, I showed him around, he asked a few questions, and a great weight was lifted from my shoulders. Joe just dealt with a load of stuff that was going on in that tent, and made it OK.

At the time of our first meeting I was too traumatised to do the usual social niceties, enquiring about past jobs and experience and so-on. And there was no need; here was a fellow who was calm and showed no fear. Details of his career have drifted to my attention over the years since, only adding to the respect with which I regard him.

Joe was centre stage when technical theatre, as we now think of it, was invented; as a stage manager and Production Manager, he realised the productions of Laurence Olivier in the late 1960's at The National Theatre (NT). He was managing the Institute of Contemporary Arts (ICA) in the mid-70's when the next generation of performers and artists challenged the old literary order with 'experimental theatre'. And over the past twenty years, as technical support of the performing arts has become a respectable occupation, and the stage has become a proper workplace, he has been at the vanguard of the education and training movement, bringing standards to the performing arts that have long been the norm in other industries.

In this book Joe shares nearly half a century of experience and teaching, and draws the conclusion that Production Management is a proper job. The Production Manager has a responsibility to his employer, to deliver product on time and on budget; to his staff and crew, to provide a safe and well organised workplace; to suppliers, to make realistic deals and fair contracts; and to the artists, to proactively work with them to realise visions and dreams, while keeping a tight grasp on all of the forgoing.

This duty of proactivity is central to his thesis. A good Production Manager is not a 'yes' man (or woman), he strives to satisfy a number of demands, only one of which is the artist's desire. A good Production Manager does not assume things are going well when they might not be, as Joe points out: "Being surprised is not managing, it's responding to stimuli - not good."

Joe says, "I always see things as separate tasks which combine to make a completed project or object." This book contains a wealth of anecdote and detail which helps us to identify the tasks, and get them done.

Simon Corder
London, July 2002

FOREWORD

All too often, at all levels of the theatre, we see people struggling against what seem to be insuperable odds. Too frequently this is because they have given a production or project too little thought or prior consideration and are working in a haphazard and disorganised way. In an endeavour to help all of us engaged in the presentation of live theatre, these words have been put down in an attempt to help us organise ourselves – and our thinking – and to apply best practices to the exercise of stagecraft.

The book is set out in separate sections. It is not meant to be read in a linear fashion; the reader may start at any point. Of course, the picture will be filled in sooner or later by reading it all. It is not meant to be a handbook for aspiring Production Managers, more an overview of the function from different perspectives. Nonetheless, much of what is included will, I hope, be of practical use not only to Production Managers, but others as well. I have tried to be impersonal, but the male pronoun does appear, and should be taken to include the female as well!

During the planning of the book, a number of anecdotes continually came to mind as illustrative of the points I was trying to make. After a period of due consideration (about 3 minutes!) I decided to set them out randomly amongst the chapters. They are set in grey boxes.

Theatre is organic. It can't all be good, so one has to be philosophical. The job of Production Management is effectively the same whether the outcome is praised or panned. If one feels one has done one's best on a poor production, that is all we can do and hope for better next time. Equally well, an unsuccessful production may involve exciting new technical developments which may well enhance future shows.

Our work is not a science. There are often different ways of achieving the required result. Also, I believe it needs to be seen, as far as possible, as fun – certainly more fun than many other jobs. The projection of an open-minded personality will do wonders in winning the co-operation of all those around you.

Europeans have been engaged in theatrical activity for over 2,500 years, and almost every developed society in history has engaged in some form of display or ritual, frequently based on faith. Religious activity and theatre share many common factors. Events take place at specific, pre-advertised times and those involved tend to wear clothes which separate them from the onlooker and identify their particular function. No great empire has flourished without a defining set of beliefs and related ceremonial. It may well be that various forms of 'theatre' preceded that of the ancient Greeks, and we are able to trace theatrical activities to the 4th Century BC.

The very fact that buildings were arranged, and places defined for actors and audience, means that people were engaged in precisely the same exercise then as those of us involved in management and staging productions are today. One can reasonably assume that the kind of conversations they were having differed little from the type of conversation we could well have with a director or producer now. The same basic performance values pertained, and many of the same reasons for something 'working' or 'not working', or for being better than something else, would also apply.

There is a mind-set that unites all experienced stage technicians. It's almost uncanny that when on tour in a foreign country people who don't speak the same language quickly grasp what has to be done. The reason must be that there is only one sensible way of doing the job and that it transcends linguistic boundaries. It may also be that we break the barrier of time as well. I'm convinced that there is a kind of generic stage technician who started work in Greece about 2,500 years ago and who hasn't retired yet. This person is inquisitive, responsible, communicative and takes pride in being part of a larger team. He is not servile and understands that his contribution is vital, but at the same time does not seek the limelight. In addition, the anti-social hours set us apart so we spend a lot of time with our peers.

Our generic stage technician also needs to be fit to handle all the artefacts of performance and to have good manual skills. Lastly, and most importantly, we need to remember that we are accumulating experience all the time. Mature practitioners will bring a greater degree of sensitivity to the work borne on past experiences. It's something not easily quantifiable, but it's certainly a factor not to be forgotten or ignored.

Also essential to the successful backstage person is the ability to function as part of a team and to do their job quickly, efficiently and to refrain from impeding the main process of the work – which is to present performers in the best possible circumstances. Good theatre technicians are rarely prima donnas and the ones most valued are those who assess the problems correctly, make the right decisions, complete work on time and enable the other departments to get on and complete their work to the overall benefit of the production. We all have the basic required mind-set and we would all, probably, have found ourselves quite useful at any time in the past, were we presented with the opportunity of travelling backwards in time!

The good technician must obviously be apprised of the received wisdom of the discipline in which he or she is engaged, but at the same time have sufficient innovative capacity to know when to throw received wisdom out of the window and reach out to experiment with new ideas. This procedure applies in cubes to Production Managers!

Over the centuries names, titles and administrative structures have changed and are still constantly evolving, as is natural with such an organic entity as theatre. A cull of programmes from the early decades of the 20th Century at London's Theatre Museum reveals hardly any individuals credited as 'Production Managers', whereas it is almost mandatory now that a production has a 'Production Manager' who is regarded by many, to all intents and purposes, as the chief technician.

There are a variety of reasons why this change has happened. The practical aspects are covered in Chapter One. However, there might have been a more subliminal force at work. WWII took a large toll on the young male workforce of Britain. The tales of some who served and then moved into the technical side of theatre just after the War, reflect how easy it was to get work having had little experience and no training. In the circumstances the management could see the logic of promoting the most experienced person to a position of overall technical responsibility with such depths of expertise. Nowadays, the word 'manager' is more important.

There are two concepts which, whether or not they are articulated, are usually applied by theatre personnel in the course of their work, Firstly, there is the understanding of the difference between principle and technology. The difference between principle and technology can be explained by considering an early human with a piece of rope. He ties a stone to this piece of rope and throws the stone, pursued by the rope, over the branch of a tree. So, when the rope is over the tree, the stone can dangle above the ground. If he pulls his end of the rope, the stone will go up and, if he perhaps flicks the rope a little to overcome the friction of the rope lying across the branch of the tree, the stone will descend. The amount of travel will be the same on either side, up or down. This basic principle remains true to this day. It is the basic principle of theatre flying, counterweighting, and all manner of systems. What has changed over the years, via the application of technology, is the tree. The tree became a pulley, probably made of wood, which was supplanted by a cast iron pulley, which was supplanted by an improved bearing, which was supplanted by a compressed fibre pulley, and so on, so that the friction over the tree has been hugely diminished, and the noise factor has been taken out and the effort required to lower or raise the stone reduced as well. However, these are all applications of newly available technology as and when they became available.

It is reasonable to say that principles are reliable. They don't change and if the basic principle behind what one is trying to do is a proven one, the probability is that, whatever is being proposed is going to work. It is important, then, for Production Management personnel to look at proposals, especially where new products are being brought forward, in this light and ask themselves whether this is something entirely new, or the application of another generation of technology to a well-worn and tested principle.

Secondly, there is the concept of incident and pattern. If something happens once, it is an incident; if it happens again, it may be the beginning of a pattern; if it happens a third time, it is almost definitely a pattern. If the event is something such as the failure of a door catch or something practical on stage, then its consistent failure will require that the stage management *do something about it*, ie: it becomes a matter for action.

Incidents and pattern abound throughout theatrical history, whether in the types of architecture, performance, or design of equipment. After WWII, considerable development was in progress to improve the playback precision and quality from 78rpm effects discs. All of this development – time, money and energy – went for nothing because of the introduction of recording tape. The ease and facility by which the sound effects for an entire play could be transferred onto one spool of tape, tucked into a pocket and carried on to the next venue, instead of lugging a chest of discs, made life easier, less subject to accidental damage, and also provided an improved 'product' for the audience.

There have been times in history when stage management or stage technicians have played a key role in the whole presentation process. Certainly there are records from Renaissance Italy which show that the people who designed the machinery for the stage, creating great effects, were paid more than those who had composed the music. In some cases, those composers are still well known today. But names of the technicians who were better paid for the original productions have been forgotten. The great thing to bear in mind is that nothing is forever and that in the short span of a century, great changes have taken place in the way we present plays, and also in the type of plays or musicals we write and put on. The factors which impinge on us to make the changes constantly change in themselves and are always likely to continue to do so. The 20th Century began within the era of the actor-manager and it ended as an era where the director, who was called a producer in the middle of the century, had become a key element in the process.

When I started work (before the old King died) in the professional theatre in 1957, one of the senior members of our crew had made his own debut in the theatre in 1903. I pondered that if, when he had started work in 1903, there had been someone with, like him, 54 years experience, then that person would have started working in 1849! So the working lives of just three individuals could span 150 years. I don't know how much of what I learned from that colleague came from his own experience or what he might have gained from those who were experienced in 1903 and passed the wisdom on to him in the early years of this century. What I do know is that when I speak to students, or give advice, today, the accumulated experience and knowledge of all those who have gone before has assisted me greatly. In the end, that is all one has to offer to those whom one either works with or to those who will continue the great traditions of people who will work backstage in the future.

This book is intended to be reasonably light-hearted, and it was written in a spirit in which I feel we should all attempt to do our work. This involves a positive attitude which says: "If we've thought it through properly, there's no reason why what we are trying to do won't work and that when it works well, it will serve the production the greatest possible advantage." We will then have succeeded in being worthy successors to our forebears.

There are a number of check lists and tables included, but these are not meant to be followed slavishly. Successful Production Management is creative and innovative, and to assume that the same paperwork will be as effective in all situations is a bad move. However, the lists and tables may help align thinking, as needs required by a new situation are in the process of being analysed.

When compiling this book, I researched all manner of lecture notes and other jottings I have made over the years and I was consistently reassured by the continuity of what I found on the yellowing pages. The basic comprehension of the work of Production Management that worked for me many years ago is, in my view, still valid. Just as important, recent experience and discussions with younger colleagues confirm that these basic premises are a good basis on which to build.

16 Production Management

Production Management is Practical

Pictured opposite is the set for The Merchant of Venice by Julia Trevelyan Oman for the National Theatre at the Old Vic.

The stage floor was raked at 1:16. The original model showed the set on an unbroken floor with the building structures compensated to vertical at the base. Either side were two loggias which were to open out to provide spaces for interior scenes. Any piece swinging from up and down to on and off on a raked floor with a vertical hinge presents a series of problems: the stresses around the turning point are too many to want to deal with.

At an early meeting, the Production Management suggested placing wedge-shaped floor pieces so that the whole stage became a series of wide steps, giving horizontal surfaces to work on and obviating the problems noted above. Good sense prevailed and the idea was quickly incorporated into the design, considerably easing the production process. One of the resultant steps is clearly visible behind the actor's knee. The draped arch behind him is able to swing forward to 'up and down' on the flat without any stress on the hinge point.

Steps are ever present in Venice so the realistic evocation of the city was, if anything, enhanced and certainly not impaired. In retrospect, one does wonder whether the proposal would have been made if we hadn't recently passed through Venice on tour.

"What happened was . . ."

Some years ago a colleague asked me to look into a project which was falling behind schedule – so far behind schedule, in fact, that it had been postponed for a year. This may not be quite as bad as it first seems because it was a summer-based project and, with time sensitive projects like that, if you don't hit the window of opportunity in one year, you do have to wait nine months before you can try again.

Nevertheless, I was asked to look into what had been going on and how things might be improved. The project suffered from having rather too many senior advisory bodies. Being in the public sector, a number of authorities of various different sizes all wished to have some input into the configuration of the outcome. The senior manager in charge was also responsible for the content of the project and was, perhaps, being asked to wear one or two hats too many.

In conversations as to how the current position was achieved, we listened to the sequences of events which had led to the initial postponement. Everything seemed entirely logical and sensible, and quite obviously no other decision bar the one that was taken could sensibly have been taken. It was only after a period of reflection, that a specific phrase kept repeating itself in my mind. Frequently, I had been told that "what happened was". A further trawl of the memory produced no recollection of someone saying "what I had decided to do was", or "what I did was". So, effectively, the management had been reactive rather than proactive. Given that there were so many agencies concerned with the outcome, there had not been any linear thinking at administrative level. The result of this was that everything that had happened, *had happened* with the knowledge and approval of senior management, but the project had *not happened*.

How different is this from a Production Manager with a director, a designer, a lighting designer and a sound designer, all operating on slightly different tangents? The Production Manager may well be the only person who can make the executive decision which will actually allow the project to proceed to conclusion. The Production Manager will have to remember that his primary duty is to his employer who is mounting the production. This recollection should serve to confirm that without management thrust no project is going to achieve fruition easily.

In my experience, the supreme example of this was the 1967 Expo at Montreal. This was an enormous undertaking for such a thinly populated, at the same time vast, country as Canada. It was only by putting a high powered senior official in charge, with powers to commandeer materials, that they were able to complete Expo on time for its opening and successful season. I was told that at one point this individual commandeered the entire supply of electrical conduit in Canada. It may have only been for a short time, and it may have pushed dozens of other building projects behind schedule, but there was a clear recognition from the Canadian Government that this high profile project was so important that nothing else should be allowed to stand in its way.

1 THE ROLE OF THE PRODUCTION MANAGER

If we consider the business of theatre to concern principally those who act upon the stage in front of an audience and those who directly assist their performance behind the scenes our assumption would have been right until perhaps just over a century ago. Within the last 100 years however we have seen a mushrooming of job functions, all connected to the theatrical production process but not necessarily involved on or even near the stage during the course of the performance. We are now very much concerned with Directors, Designers, Lighting Designers, Administrators and Consultants – all these people have enormous input into the performance and yet after the first night, other than for pastoral care, their responsibilities are handed over to those who run the performance. The creators are free to move on to wider fields.

The Production Manager is one of these more recent personnel. We hear of Technical Managers or Co-ordinators, all technical supremos of one kind or another in various different types of theatre. For the purposes of the discussion that follows we should define what we mean here by Production Manager. We will consider the Production Manager being the person who gathers all the work of the various disciplines together in order that they arrive on the stage at the correct time and in the right order. He acts as a liaison between all the different manufacturing processes, and the design personnel. The performers and the staff who work or operate the show also fall under his influence because the PM will have had a role in defining the dynamic by which the performance flows.

The job function developed as a result of forces operating from different practical directions, as well as the sociological theory outlined in the Foreword. One needs to consider how things were done before the changes started to occur and to chart the change so as to gain a complete picture. There are many authoritative books on the art of Stage Managing and the responsibilities involved. Most people within our theatrical framework have a positive view as to what a stage manager does, and does not, have to do. As the years have moved forward stage managers are required to take an ever closer look at the rehearsal process and to liaise more closely with the Director. The stage manager's functions have increased as the demands of the acting company have increased upon him.

Clear the mind and think of a theatre without a designer or a director. Star performers would select from a stock of scenery those pieces which they considered most appropriate. For grander occasions a scenic artist would be engaged to paint a new woodland scene or Aladdin's cave. Because the formatting of settings was itself formalised into perspective wings, it was possible for several different scenic artists to do different scenes of the same show. Once the promoter had decided to spend the money, no other decision taking process was really necessary once the scenic artists had been commissioned.

Some theatres, especially the repertories which started in the early years of the 20th Century, had a stock of flats which would be washed and repainted. The designers frequently drew a simple ground plan and then got out the bits of stock they needed which, when painted, were placed onstage according to the plan. Resident stage managers or stage directors held sway in charge of crews who moved the wood and canvas scenery about. Many theatres had their own painting facility either on the back wall or in a workshop adjacent to the stage where scenic artists worked during the day, leaving before the evening performance. Communication was easy, being direct and verbal. Skilled people simply got on with what they were good at.

The increasing complexity of scenic design and the increasing number of materials being used within the construction of scenery and properties has a big impact. This trend really got going in the 1950's, but in fairness it has to be said that World War II did put a block in the way of progress for a period. The change is such that the traditional method of producing scenery hardly applies today. Each design has to be dealt with on its merits and given individual attention.

More specialised skills are now frequently required. The skill of the scenic artist is perhaps less demanding in the sense of reproducing less figurative work, but more in assessing which method will actually produce the desired visual effect upon whatever material has been chosen. Be it the use of caustics, acids or paints sprayed, daubed, dragged, scraped, pushed, shoved or whatever onto the material - these are qualitative judgements – they require time and consultation and management.

The traditional stage manager was not able within the constraint of his time to service adequately the new demands. Therefore the need arose for someone who would be able to devote his time to liaising between craft disciplines and designers. He may initially have been called a Stage Director but eventually the word Production Manager came into the theatrical vocabulary. The Production Manager has always been conceived as being related to a production rather than a building as with a resident stage manager. Production Managers in name are already being superseded by other titles, but whatever the case, most producing theatre companies have someone on their staff who fulfils the kind of function we are considering.

The job of Production Manager will vary depending upon the kind of theatre company the Production Manager finds himself with. We should consider here some quite different areas, and at the same time look at how the job might vary in terms of responsibility.

Production Managers in large subsidised theatres, those 'Centres of Excellence' which are the pinnacle of our national dramatic or operatic achievement, are able to draw upon skilled staff within the establishment of their company. They also have the advantage that the company will be providing a framework of workshops in which to carry out quite complicated constructions or decorations. These will either be within the building or even in a separate facility. Some companies find it more economic to sub-contract scenic and other construction, but in most cases there is enough resource for space not to be a prime problem.

Within these large national companies in the UK, because of their relatively high levels of grant aid and, to a certain extent the negotiating powers of Trades Unions, staff tend to remain in post for a long time, if not for the greater part of their working life in some cases. There is a visible career path that can be pursued. This level of experience within the staff is a boon to a Production Manager. And he should know which members of the staff are able to undertake what sort of work. Looking at a proposed task stretching in front of him he should be able to tell which of the people he knows will get the best results in the best possible time.

With this establishment around him, the job becomes a straightforward one of assessing how the proposed production can be encompassed within the constraints of the staff and the other work taking place. By staying in their posts over years and developing relationships between themselves, staff are to a large extent self-contained, or become that way, and do not demand too much from the Production Manager. They already know the system by which the theatre works and what quality of work will be acceptable. People in these companies who achieve HoD ranking often tend to have been working in the system for some years, rather than having entered laterally. Job security means that they can assess situations without prejudice to themselves or without looking perhaps to potential additional earnings accruing over the period of production, which can be the case elsewhere.

Production Management in large subsidised theatres, then, is to some extent like generalship within the military. The system in the army or the military exists where the non-commissioned officers (NCOs) tend to run day-to-day affairs, leaving the strategic planning to the Commissioned Officers. The Senior NCOs in the theatre are the HoDs; the Production Manager is perhaps at a tactical decision level amongst the commissioned ranks. The analogy holds, insofar that in larger organisations the HoDs are people of responsibility who are able to run their departments and undertake the work that is given to them without passing problems upwards to a Production Manager.

So upon receiving instructions to carry out production, the Production Manager's job is one of liaison with the various HoDs – scenery, metal, props, paint and so on. A time scale has to be established as well as some kind of estimate of the materials to be used (however, it must be said that in the larger subsidised theatres budgetary considerations don't always make great inroads into the concept of a play as envisaged by a Designer or Director). Additionally, he will then have to contact and the HoDs of the crews on the stage who will have to handle the material as it comes forward. Additional items may also need to be purchased from the outside. These will have to be specified, costed, and suppliers contracted.

In the main, if all the required services are available within the company, the Production Manager's job remains one of internal communication and monitoring progress as it passes through the workshops towards the completed product ready to go onstage.

A different situation exists in a regional producing theatre. Here again, you may also have all the various disciplines 'in house' – you will probably have a workshop, prop maker, and wardrobe, but not to the same extent as in a bigger company. In recent times reps have started to share costs by touring productions from one theatre to another – a rare occurrence where an economy measure increases the potential for more people to enjoy the art. This reduces the number of new productions in some cases. You usually have a fixed period of production – four-weekly or whatever – and this implies that almost anything you are confronted with should be built in that given period. However, some theatres are not sufficiently well-blessed with storage space to be able to build sets in advance and hold them until they are ready to go onto the stage.

Repertory theatres have to dismantle what is on the stage, bring the new work from the workshop to the stage, and take back to the workshop what they require of the dismantled pieces ready for reconstruction into other shapes and forms.

The Production Manager in a rep theatre, I feel is a bit more of a *pater-familias* as opposed to a brigadier. Because there are fewer people in the organisation the personal relationships tend to become more focused and it is quite advantageous that people get on well with each other in more than just a professional sense. Sensible 'father figuring' can often persuade people to do something which is perhaps slightly beyond their average capacity or ability and which is going to create a certain additional work-load, albeit for a shorter period. In repertory theatre, unlike some repertoire houses, the Production Manager is usually responsible for hiring SMs, DSMs and their assistants as well. Therefore anyone operating in the non-acting or directing area / technical area of the theatre tends to be responsible to the Production Manager.

The small 'nuclear' team is ideal. The Production Manager must have people who have all the skills and who, sometimes with the addition of extra labour, can produce what is required. His budgeting will be a lot more complicated insofar that rep theatres generally have much tighter budgetary limitations than bigger organisations. This is not to say they cannot produce good work – but it does demand a positive relationship between the Production Manager and his staff, his director and his designers. Again, rep theatres often tend to use the same designers regularly. The kind of relationship which develops between the designers, HoDs and Production Manager will be beneficial to all. A sensible designer is not going to ask an HoD to produce something which they know will cause difficulty. The Production Manager's job entails ensuring that people have got what they need in terms of equipment and materials and monitoring the work that is happening. We don't want to hear that something isn't right, or is late, for the want of a certain tool or type of glue.

The Production Manager is usually the person more responsible for assuring that supplies are brought in. He therefore has less time to spend on working out technical details than he might wish. On the other hand he may find that the designer has more time. In a larger theatre the designer may be involved in doing three or four or more sets in other theatres – sometimes in theatres which are not even in the UK – and this could take him away for weeks at a time during the production period.

The most difficult kind of Production Management is that involved in the commercial theatre, especially in the so-called 'West End'. Here one has a situation where one is completely off base – there is no 'home' base. The theatres in the West End rent themselves to Producing Managements for the mounting of productions. The managements frequently do not have their own stores, workshops or painters – the entire structure is set up entirely for the mounting of a particular play. The Production Manager's job, therefore, when given the designs for a new play, is to identify who amongst the available manufacturers of scenery or properties or painters or costumes is going to make each individual item that is required. Even more complicated is the necessity to ensure that constructor Y is aware that constructor X is making something that has to fit over or under or next to something made by constructor Y, and to ensure that when the fit up takes place that everything will fit together and that there will no be delays in the production process. This leads to a complex contractual situation which is dealt with in Chapter 4.

All managements are keen to open shows in the West End as soon as practically possible after moving into the theatre, because they are paying rent from the moment the fit-up commences. They do not receive any recoup on the expenditure until the revenue from the box office starts to mature, and this doesn't happen until they actually admit the first audience. Therefore the time-scale and planning for West End work has to be considerably more detailed. Every hour of every person employed will cost money. This is a different situation from one where you have the strength of staff mentioned earlier. Also the main thing to remember about purely commercial work is the fact that the people involved in the production will not have anything like the close working knowledge of each other when compared to either a rep or large subsidised theatre.

Commercial productions are put together on one-off project basis and contractors are selected according to their estimate being satisfactory or their known ability to complete the work within a given time scale. It is impossible to predict which ones will be engaged until you actually get into the exercise and you cannot therefore guarantee the close co-operation built on long term acquaintance between the departments that you get in permanent establishments. In order to cover this 'gap' the Production Manager's workload is correspondingly increased. It is up to him to make these missing liaisons function by making the intentions of each contractor clear to the other contractors and also to the theatre staff and making the scheduling of the 'get in' clear to everyone else involved, including stage management, design team, senior management and hauliers. He must also ensure that the work is completed in the various contractors' workshops at approximately the time you need it in the theatre – otherwise you face the problem of where to store it!

From personal experience the Production Manager's work in the West End is a lot less rewarding, and considerably more arduous because of consistently having to maintain or develop relationships between people who either do not know each other or if they have worked together in the past it could have been many years ago. Some commercial managements maintain their own Production Manager and, by dint of forward planning, are able to mount productions over a period of years using, by and large, the same contractors. This helps solve some of the potential problems mentioned above. However, not all West End plays are mounted as a result of long term strategic planning! West End Production Managers clearly earn their cash in a more pressured way than those involved in rep and subsidised theatres.

On the other hand it must be said that most scenic and other contractors are extremely competent – the world in which they live is sufficiently cut-throat for them not to be able to survive unless they have developed an efficient operation. Working in the West End with freelance professional contractors who have been provided with minimal information may well result in an extremely fine finished product, because they have developed enough relevant expertise.

There are many more facets to Production Management. The so-called 'fringe' has a need for the function too. In very small companies it can become almost a one-man band, but the basics still apply in this microcosm. The disorganised one-man band will achieve far less and cause more grief to colleagues than the one who finds time whilst painting the walls to analyse the overall developing situation.

These, then, are brief descriptions of the differences between the Production Manager's job in different types of theatre.

Nothing remains the same in the theatre for very long. It is organic as we all know. Nevertheless it is important to indicate that there are quite significant differences in the way one approaches the job and the help you could expect to get. The latter point is quite key and crucial in the commercial sector where private money is being invested. The Production Manager's ability to wave the financial big stick, i.e. budgetary constraint – is considerably enhanced. With rep this ability is in the middle range and in the larger subsidised theatres I would suggest his ability to use this particular method of control is at its least 'efficient'.

By controlling the purse the Production Manager has the final answer to most of the problems presented – it can either be done or not be done – according to the amount of money that is left unspent in the budget. He may, of course, have to go back to the producing management and suggest that the expenditure of additional funds might be beneficial to the production in the long run.

Where Do We Come From?

It is difficult and perhaps presumptuous to state from where Production Managers should be drawn. The work they do covers so many different disciplines that it would be an invidious decision to have to take. Perhaps the best thing to do is to suggest some of the types of skill and knowledge required.

I know of a case in Europe wheare a man left a career in nuclear science to become an extremely successful theatrical Production Manager in a large theatre. Broad technical skills probably led most Production Managers to where they are today. However their success will depend on how good they are at other aspects as management skill allied to one technical skill is the key factor in successful Production Management. Now let us look at the various different types of expertise that will be called upon as part of the work of being a Production Manager.

Let us consider the immediate position before one takes up a position as a Production Manager as there is no given training format for PM's as such. Because there are established routes to Stage Management and some of the technical disciplines, many people choose one of these paths into the profession. Having got there they may have a degree of success. If they rise rapidly or develop a reputation for reliability then the opportunity for promotion will occur. Because of the importance now bestowed on Production Managers the chance will usually come to individuals who have demonstrated skill, energy and judgement in their originally chosen discipline. Experience of the process is often seen as a reason for promoting. One cannot think of many instances where someone without experience successfully acquires a job as a PM in a company where he has never worked before. So we have to assume that the new PM will have greater expertise in some areas than others. Their degree of understanding of the work of colleagues will effect their decision making, and success will only come to those who can take an all-embracing view.

The one technical skill which is pre-emptive for Production Managers has to be scale drawing. It's not just the skill, as they say, it's how you do it. The ability should extend to being able to generate drawings from a set of onsite measurements. You soon learn which dimensions are truly important. You also learn to assess situations onsite in respect of what you want your drawing to show. After all, it is being done to carry information to others in the team. As you take the dimensions you should be developing in your head a picture of the plan and the section as well and how they relate to each other. Sections have a habit of varying if the angle of the stage floor changes and these can effect the plan.

Remember you can't trust anybody. Rarely was a plan presented from a venue or a designer in which immediate implicit trust could be placed. After all, it could have been done by someone about as highly skilled as oneself! Frequently the particular facet you need is not well described. So one should take the time and feel more secure with the home grown variety.

I learnt the fundamentals of this at The Bristol Old Vic Theatre School. The key measurements were noted as:

> height of proscenium
> width of proscenium
> depth of stage
> width of stage
> height of stage
> Prosc line to front lip
> Front lip to front row
> Distance up or down from front row eyeline to stage level.

From these you can get a good overall sense of the space – something on which to build.

There is another truism punted about when you learn geometry. That is that a line *per se* has no thickness. Of course it does – I can see it. So one realises that no matter how precise we are and no matter how thin the line on a scale drawing at 1:25, only part of it can be right. Any human error in taking measurements from a line on a plan will multiply exponentially at full size. For this reason I have found points rather than lines to be more reliable for consistency, often the upstage corners of the proscenium. The lines of the set appear on the plan to tell you what its going to look like but they needn't be used for measuring purposes.

There is an inbuilt random factor in a manually generated drawing. This comes from the angle of the pen to the edge against which it is being drawn. Our joints, wrists, elbows and shoulders, rotate or work in single plane angles and are not designed for parallel movement. The computer generated drawing obviates this but the line still remains a line with its potential inaccuracy. In the CAD case the ease with which the lines can be produced can lead to too many lines which can blur the message of the drawing.

Knowing that errors multiply, it is always best, for instance, to measure every flying position from the same point – ideally something solid like the prosc wall. When the measurements are transferred to the drawing each will be of equal value, i.e. any slight error made on one will have no bearing on any other. If the prosc wall is irregular in any way the measurements need to be related to the stage floor some other way. In the last resort a plumb line dropped from a convenient centre pulley will provide a datum point on the stage floor which can be related to something tangible at deck level.

Drawing the stage, or a set, somehow seems to bring you closer too it. Perhaps more so with sets a sense of its key points emerges. This often helps the process of planning the fit up or the order in which you will want to do the deading. It may also show up areas of flexibility, useful in the next round of chats with lighting and sound designers.

Parkinson's Law, where work expands to fill the time allowed, is reasonably well known. As useful, but less well known, is the Peter Principle. The Peter Principle states that people get promoted to their level of incompetence. So, to assume that a skilled HoD will translate into a good Production Manager is not always a good idea. If the management and necessary inter-personal skills don't emerge, a rather stagnant approach is likely to result. However, in more regional situations, this can seem a good option for managements because it offers the opportunity of promoting, rewarding and retaining a well-regarded staff member.

The Peter Principle can obviously have a negative effect. In some cases where personnel have passed mid-career and see no room for advancement, they become protective. If they are employed in a large organisation, this protectiveness can lead to not making 'waves', i.e. stick to what you know. This syndrome needs to be recognised and once identified, the Production Manager's inter-personal skills will now be sorely tested as he leads, small step by small step, towards the embracing of a newish idea or method. The key is to enthuse and drive the notion of mutual satisfaction with a team succeeding in what it set out to do.

Although not directly part of the Peter Principle we must be aware of the impact of change, especially age. As a Production Manager responsible for running a team these are important factors. For instance, if all your HoDs are working well together in the fullness of their youth, all will be well. The years will pass, some will age faster than others, some will respond better to changing technology. It cannot be assumed that the team will continue to be as effective indefinitely.

Production Managers need a knowledge of people: what makes them tick, why they are involved in the theatre which is, after all, a hard task-mistress, what they are seeking out of it and what they are putting into it? This may sound as if one should be an amateur psychotherapist – but this may be partially necessary in order to estimate peoples' ability to carry out work and tasks given to them. It is useful to understand what it is that motivates them to do it. Some people require one kind of encouragement, some another. Others work better under pressure. Some people work better within an overall work plan into which every piece of work activity is delicately slotted and they are not required to change their pace. Some people work better when in fury or anger with someone else. Some people work better when praised, cajoled or nudged into producing good work.

If a Production Manager is to get the best out of his assembled team he should be able to convey careful advice about the individuals to people such as the designer, costume designer, lighting designer, or director – pointing out to them that this particular person may require a certain type of handling and another require another. This is not to say that the team are not professional or that they cannot be relied upon to do their job, but I think it is fair to say that within the theatre, people who produce their best work in their own best emotional surroundings, produce something better than a purely professionally turned out job. People who are treated correctly towards their own motivations usually produce better work faster than someone who is simply working on a professional tread mill.

Then there is the knowledge of style. I do not believe that anyone can enter into any kind of conversation with a director or designer unless they have a knowledge of style.

Many years ago, whilst I was attending the Bristol Old Vic Theatre School, the Principal, Duncan Ross, almost off-the-cuff and not in the context of a formal class, gave us a little homily about 'style'. It remains stuck in my head. It was probably the most important and useful piece of advice I have ever been given. From that day to this I continue to apply it. I found it especially useful when having those discussions with designers where concept and reality meet up. I will share it with you.

Imagine a line. It has two ends: one is called formal and the other illusion. Illusion is easy because it is the illusion of reality. We know we are watching a performance that has been prepared for us, everything we see or hear is highly realistic. An extreme example might be an outdoor production of *Love's Labours Lost* in a woody park, late on a summer's afternoon, where the audience perambulate among the performers. Everything fits – the location, the light, the birdsong – even the fresh air. We have slipped into another world of reality, almost as voyeurs. Formal, on the other hand, is where we behave in preset patterns which we didn't devise. A good example is the State Opening of Parliament. People dress up as Black Rod or Heralds and walk about the Palace of Westminster, sometimes backwards, and hit doors with their sticks. A ritual. Just as when one goes to a formal church service we don't expect the priest to come out with a whole new twist on the story of Christ. We expect our sustaining beliefs to be upheld.

Without thinking, our body language changes according to what we are wearing. Women cannot but agree when it is suggested that there are body positions they can adopt which they would not dream of doing whilst wearing a skirt. Men, as well, tend to cut out extraneous movement when a dinner jacket is donned. So, we do have an inbuilt comprehension of style. Now its application can be explored.

The objective is satisfied when nothing jars the senses of the audience, breaking into their suspension of disbelief. A designer knows that as we become more formal we can involve a degree of surrealism as well. There are endless examples, but it is best to accustom oneself to applying the concept. It is the best means of drawing the disparate strands together. Almost unthinkingly, one finds oneself saying, "But if we do this here, it won't fit with that there," etc, etc. The great thing is that if the concept is sound, the resultant conversations are usually very positive.

This applies, then, to everything: actors, set, costumes, and especially the dynamic of the performance. How, for instance, could one have a 'high tech' set *and* long, laborious scene changes. Something might have to give to make it work. It is here, too, that the Production Manager's technical expertise can come into play by blending the needs together so that the result is the seamless, problem-free production. If a Production Manager doesn't want to engage in this part of the creative process, then they are missing out on one of the most satisfying parts of the job.

Most productions, if they are to be successful, gather together all departments at some pre-arranged point along the line. This will ensure that there is an homogeneity of style. We can think of productions that have not worked and, if we think back, we can say 'yes because the light was operating in another style from the set'. If the set was naturalistic it would normally depend upon some kind of naturalistic light to make it function and vice-versa. A Production Manager should have a knowledge of this type of style which enables him to offer sensible instructions to the people employed to create his hardware. If he cannot articulate the 'why' of something then he is not properly able to indicate what is needed – the style in which something is to be carried out. It enables him to answer questions.

The styles he must also have knowledge of are those of architecture or decoration. There are styles which are in most cases researchable, available in reference libraries or elsewhere. It is useful, naturally, to carry in one's head some styles, as an bank of knowledge. But knowledge of more precise theatrical styles is something which becomes an 'essential' in terms of being able to communicate. For instance, when in the early phase of production, one is discussing the broad aspects of how the stage is to appear, you frequently find yourself asking, 'is this a show where we see the lanterns?' You ask this because you see a style of set being developed and, as we know, models of sets are not always presented with borders, etc. You might feel that perhaps within a slightly more formal context that the lanterns might be visible. On the other hand it may be that we are moving towards naturalism and the lanterns need not be visible. This particular point is invidious as these days we are quite used to seeing lanterns FOH, therefore the image of lanterns on stage is one which has to be carefully thought through in terms the of style of a production.

Managing

Managing is difficult thing to define in that it is a combination of skill, budgeting, organising and time scheduling. It is an ability to predict what is going to happen and have pre-prepared responses for all foreseen eventualities. It is an ability to devise in advance a plan/pattern of events, and so organise the people involved so that the pattern of events actually works as conceived. If something is quoted as being 'badly managed' it usually means that things have become haphazard and there is no evidence of there ever being any overall plan. I feel that successful Production Manager has to have some kind of vision of the various stages of a production process and fit up. If you do not have this kind of concept in your mind you are totally unable to evaluate whether or not you are either in advance of or behind schedule. If you cannot make that evaluation you cannot make changes according to the pressures as they arrive. You cannot say, "Shall we work on for an extra couple of hours to get this finished?" In this instance, if you are ahead of schedule, the answer is "no", so why waste more money? If you are behind schedule, the answer must be "yes, we must", in order to claw back time to the position we should have been at the end of this particular day.

Management can be seen as an ability to plan and in doing so create circumstances that enable the plan can be materialised. This is not simply a question of achieving hardware on the stage; it is also a case of ensuring that adequate staff from all the various disciplines are on hand in adequate numbers at the right time to do the job that is being planned to be done at that time. This, some people find, can simply be done in their heads, whilst other people may find it necessary to put it down on paper and make fairly detailed plans which can then be circulated to others. Referring back to what has been said already, in a West End situation where the time-planning has to be very sensitively tuned, the Production Manager must make all staff aware of the times they are expected to be working and the times when they are not expected to be working.

The production is a collation of people and they may not have gone through this process with each other before. In a theatre with its own staff, there tends to evolve a pattern of work for productions whereby the Production Manager merely needs to note any changes in the agreed pattern and make the personnel aware that this one is only slightly different to the normal criteria.

Management also involves the question of understanding the process by which people interact. Within management terms in the theatre most of our work takes place under what is broadly described as project-based management. People on each particular project are given functions and they will normally tend to fulfil the same function on each production/project as it comes by. In the theatre we don't often find people moving from being Master Carpenter to Property Maker to Milliner because we demand a certain high level of specialisation in those fields. However, it is not inconceivable that in the future the alternative management system known as Matrix Management may appear in the area – shall we say the non-commissioned officers. People may then function in different areas of different productions, either to keep their minds fresh or to correctly share the balance of a work-load over a longer period such as one year.

Another, and quite key area where a Production Manager must have at least some working knowledge is of how and why buildings 'stand up'. Very frequently, and it has always been so, we are asked to make additions, knock holes in or out of or into parts of the buildings we are working in, to change their shape, or to add new lighting structure or suspension systems. All of these have a bearing on the building and its ability to carry various types of load at various different points of its structure. I am not suggesting that a Production Manager should have to have an intimate knowledge of the building characteristics but certainly he should be aware of the various different types of building method that have existed during the last century or so – being the period in which most of the theatres we work in were built. Brick buildings have different characteristics to pre-stressed concrete buildings or wooden structures. Wooden grids obviously have different characteristics from metal grids, and so on. I believe that a good working knowledge of the types of construction are invaluable to the Production Manager in his ability to make the correct decision when it comes to altering buildings, which we so often have to do for new productions.

As the years have gone by, and almost surreptitiously, the word 'management' has become more important than the word 'production'. Increasingly, it seems that management skills are those which the individual needs more and more whilst, at the same time, retaining a degree of technical expertise.

This was specifically brought home to me whilst teaching a summer school. We had divided the entrants into those with some experience and those with very little. This enabled us to push the more experienced individuals a little further and be more demanding. We set the group (about 14 or 15 persons) the task of mounting a production of about 15 minutes in length in 2½ days; at the same time they had to devise their own script and scenario. Many of those involved were drawn from management or professional backgrounds and they produced a delightful, largely sound and vision (no dialogue) piece. It looked at various different means of travel from the earliest times to the present day in a series of cameos picked out by lighting as well as the use of some film and smoke for the rocket launch which ended the story.

With guidance, they managed the task extremely well. It was during the de-briefing that one of the students said that the exercise had reminded him of the kind of thing being done in management training courses. This of course is perfectly correct because a theatre production is basically 'a project' in industrial terms.

There is ample evidence that people in the theatre are amongst the finest project managers to be found anywhere. The inflexibility of the time-frame geared towards a specific opening date, plus the complexity of the tasks, means that whether they consider it or not, theatre people are engaged in a very highly pressured, complex project operation. Many of us who work in the theatre have had disturbing experiences when collaborating with people who are not used to the process. This frequently happens when one needs to acquire something from a specialist firm who normally deal in another field. We rarely get the sense of immediate response and reaction from those 'outside' as one does from those whose specialism is creating things for the theatre.

There is also the dilemma of the generation gap. Because the profession is relatively new, many first generation PMs simply used their individual career experience – there being no role models to follow. However they would have all been valued technicians in the first place and had the respect of their peers. The big question now is how we relate when we are young to those who are old – and how we relate when we are old to those who are young? This is not as simple as it sounds. Before delving into the subject one has to say that person who tells you that he's been doing this job for thirty years etc etc and therefore needs respect triggers every available alarm bell. This type of statement can mask a narrow mind that is resistant to change.

Young Production Managers will inevitably work with designers and others who are much older, with vast wells of experience. There is much to be learnt from them, especially in the field of style. In many cases the more experienced colleague may have done it before in a certain way, which may be well worth considering. As our own experiences multiply and our confidence improves with age, younger designers will start appearing! In many cases they may feel that they want our advice, especially if one's own reputation is one of being reasonable and positive. The most awkward circumstances in my memory are from the early days when the entire team was young. Despite outward appearances there lurked a touch of insecurity about how we were all going to mesh together. After all, it was only our entire careers that were at stake!

The more you do it, the better you are likely to get, or so they say. The more times you have seen something, the more times you are likely to predict correctly the result. Therefore use your judgement to inform the process towards the most successful possible conclusion.

The Production Manager's relationships vary according to the people he finds around him. Understanding the nature of these relationships will contribute to making his life either successful or unsuccessful. If you understand your position within the broad spectrum of society you tend normally to be happier than if you do not. So let us look first in this chapter at the relationship with THE MANAGEMENT. It is quite important that the Production Manager first of all ascertains at exactly what level the management expect him to function. And when I say at what level I mean he should ascertain as soon as possible what kind of decision is he allowed to take. This will vary from individual to individual as far as managers are concerned. When you say what kind of decision is someone going to be allowed to take, you are really saying how much money am I allowed to put at risk, without reference elsewhere.

It is a very difficult situation for all concerned if you find that you are having to refer elsewhere. Managements should be aware of this as well as Production Managers. If a Production Manager is not allowed or given the freedom to communicate with any kind of supplier without having to refer back to management this diminishes his standing in the face of the supplier and also slows up the process of getting the finished product. Therefore I believe that the Production Manager and his Management should have a relationship which is founded on trust and also one which is reasonably close and whereby there is frequent and amiable contact so that there is no feeling of separation – merely one of co-operation.

A management mounting a production has many things to think about beyond the Production Manager area i.e. publicity, rehearsal rooms, casting, etc. So the Production Manager's job, in order to maintain the management's trust, is to ensure that things are being correctly handled, that they, the management, are not having things withheld from them, that they can trust that he will bring forward problems as and when they arise and discuss problems which need to be resolved with the management.

If there are to be rather extensive changes in design or emphasis, things happen in the rehearsal process which will quite materially effect a product in terms of shape or design or cast. At this point the Production Manager must sit down with the management and explain that this is going to cost just a little bit more money because it needs a change – and do we value the new idea that much, or this is what the new idea costs. Do you want to push it that far? By taking the management into a decision such as this spreads the corporate weight of the responsibility for taking that decision. This is not to say that the Production Manager should not take that decision but if it is at variance from the concept that had originally been brought forward then I believe that there should be as wide a view as possible.

To sum up then, the Production Manager's relationship with the management must be established, if it is a new one, very early in the process of production. If it is a normal producing company he should ascertain who in the management structure is normally the most responsible or likely person to take decisions affecting productions. This can prove difficult as titles in the theatre do not always indicate who is the key person within any structure. Personalities do tend to play rather a large role. But given the fact that the Production Manager is able to assess the individuals with whom he is placed in juxtaposition in a management structure he should try to work out which is the key link in the chain structure which is immediately above him, and then the one above that, to develop a relationship such as we have stated above and then do the best to maintain the relationship by keeping all the information freely available and above board.

The role is a complex one. It stands as an interface between the creators, the fabricators, the funders and the performers. It demands openess, fairness, and above, all imagination. It suits an enquiring mind open to ideas, innovation and change. An understanding of the dynamics of performance and audience reaction will help guide the conversation as productions move from concept phase to reality. The ability to project an upbeat attitude will help enormously.

Lastly, because most Production Managers have achieved the position from one of the technical or stage management disciplines, they should remember what they used to expect from the Production Managers they must have worked under. In the worst case they can strive to avoid causing the kind of grief to others that they themselves might have suffered from dithering Production Managers in the past! Uneasy lies the head that wears a crown – sometimes.

2 RELATING TO DESIGNERS

Relationships with designers are, in relation to the terms of the finished visual product on stage, the most crucial of all the relationships the Production Manager has to develop. The designer is the person who is making the hard line decisions about the style and general appearance of what is due to happen on the stage. A Production Manager should want to develop a relationship of mutual respect with a designer, especially if they are working within a company or if, over the years, they collaborate frequently.

It is crucial that the Production Manager has an understanding not only of the play, opera or ballet – but also of the style in which it is to be done (see Chapter 1). He must convey his knowledge or understanding to the designer so that the designer will feel able to converse freely with the Production Manager about the needs of the production in aesthetic terms. Some designers are considerably more technically proficient in theatre technology than others. It would not be doing the late Michael Knight an injustice to say that he was one of that breed of designers who felt that he had to have technical control over all the designs on stage, and of all the suppliers and contractors involved in a creation. Because of his own well-equipped mind, he was able to create some very complicated, even astounding, productions – especially in the area of complex mechanical scenery. However, were he not so well-equipped technically and wanted to design within his own technical limitations, it is likely that his work would have been rather different. Other designers have the refreshing attitude of saying, effectively, 'It should look like this, but how you do it is up to you . . .'

If the designer's job is to produce the concept of what is needed on the stage, then the Production Manager's job arises from that concept – to produce a viable finished product. This he can do if he has adequate technical knowledge and organisational skills to implement and even supplement the designer's vision as jointly understood.

I preferred to work with designers who presented their ideas or models and allowed the Production Management to sort out how it was all to be achieved. Obviously, close liaison has to be maintained and the designer kept informed as to one's intentions. No-one will ever then be able to say later, "I was never told – if I had been, I never would have agreed to it!" The more the designer senses one is in sympathy with his work, the easier the situation becomes. Remember, too, that designers, by the nature of their employment, aren't always available on a day-to-day basis, so the Production Manager will be fielding a lot of the immediate calls for clarification.

When one is dealing with repertoire in a large working theatre, we should in the earliest phase of discussion indicate any kind of strictures which may exist, either financial or physical. I believe that these ground rules must be put forward in as sensible a way as possible and be well argued and well reasoned. It is not, in most of our natures, easy to accept things that are laid down simply because they are rules – but if there are whys and wherefores attached to them we begin to see that they have some level of acceptability. It there are strictures, it is our job to convince the designer that there are reasons for them which are viable and valid.

It is always the job of the Production Manager to assist the designer towards gaining as close a representation of the design concept on stage as possible. If the designer does not feel the Production Manager has this as a cardinal interest then he will not have an adequate level of confidence in the Production Manager. And if he does not have that, then the communication systems will break down and there are liable to be problems at the crucial stage of production as the set starts to be erected in the theatre.

The relationship with the designer may be a more personal one, perhaps, than with the management, because it is to do with the product in terms of the needs and wants of the product. It is this closeness and the sharing of needs which will bring these two job functions close enough so that there is such a clear understanding that the Production Manager may be able to take valued decisions secure in the knowledge that what he is doing will gain the approbation of the designer. The designer will know that the Production Manager has sufficient understanding of the production that he is likely to take the right decisions – even those decisions regarding paint or visual aspects of the show if the designer is unavailable. If the designer cannot feel confident of this, then the bond is broken. It is an absolutely vital thing and only comes from experience and the knowledge of the script and its inerpretation, supplemented by early conversations with the designer.

The relationship with the designer can start before anything is even put on paper. If you have adequate warning as to who is to be fulfilling the various functions then designer and Production Manager can join together early on and discuss the broad parameters of the situation before actually putting pen to drawing board or cutting knife into the model card. This will hopefully result in a concept that is not a surprise to the Production Manager or constructor because they too will have been forewarned. If everyone has a clear working knowledge, then the likelihood of a trouble-free production period is enhanced. If the relationship with the designer is one of trust and mutual understanding of the needs of the production, and similar mutual respect for each other's role, the combined wits of the two can act in concert.

All of us in the theatre have varied personalities and react in different ways to pressure applied from different types of source. Hopefully the Production Manager, by a sensible approach and by adopting a sensible plan, as mentioned elsewhere, will be able to assure the designer that things are on schedule and that there is no cause for concern. Although I'm aware some people work well under pressure I sincerely believe that most people take their best decisions when they have had a chance to consider as many possible factors bearing upon that decision as possible. The increased use of high speed electronic communications has put pressure on recipients – people want instant answers. The problem is that the instant answer may not be the best one. Sometimes it is best to pause for thought. After all, if the respondent is so desperate for an answer, he may not be managing his own situation too well! When one is in a panic-stricken situation one patently does not have this kind of time and can make a decision which is either based on very little thought or prevailing emotion. This can sometimes lead to problems further downstream.

We are all the same. There is usually something in a body of work which particularly pleases us, even though we may not be saying so openly. The Production Manager's understanding of style becomes a really useful tool. At the moment when a designer, a new model and a Production Manager meet. If the proposals have inherent problems then suggestions to solve them can be directed away from the areas closest to the designer's heart. Therefore, the designer should not feel that what pleases him most is threatened.

Communication is a much bandied word. The work produced by a designer – models, drawings, etc. – are communications. They are there for others to follow as instructions. The question is, do we all understand what is being communicated? The very language we speak is open to interpretation. The different usages of English in different English speaking countries is already recognised and, as time passes, the differences will increase, so that English becomes more of a root language on which newer dialects grow. The conversation between an American designer and an English scenic artist can be very interesting. But the Production Manager must be absolutely certain that all is 100% clear. *It is not a good idea to assume anything.*

Some designers offer more than others, so the job of ensuring that all the fabricators and decorators have got it right tends to vary considerably. One recalls a very well known designer producing a model consisting of cut-out dyeline elevations pasted, unpainted, on to card. When asked about the style of decoration the answer was 'Empire style'. All the scenic artist had to do was pick the right empire! In some cases, designers already know or have worked with, a costumier or painter. If that liaison was successful, they will have already developed the kind of shorthand that is needed. It can be a laborious process, but it has to be done. One way is to ask a designer if the prop maker is fully briefed and, at the same time, confirm his instruction. Then, one should independently ask the prop maker and see if the same answer comes back. If it doesn't then an excuse has to be found for a further meeting. The overriding objective has got to be that nobody should, even for a second, be unsure of what is wanted.

A lot has been written here about set designers. They are not alone. Sound and lighting designers are all part of the team too. Lighting and sound equipment on the stage has grown exponentially, rather more than scenery in recent years. This has the effect of creating a space auction. If the performance space is seen as a volume, then each of the designers is seeking to use some of it. So far, so good. But what if two or more want the same chunk of the space? This is where the understanding comes in. This is where the Production Manager senses that what may be pivotal to someone's concept may seem less to someone else's. Again, if *everyone* has to compromise, then the whole may be adversely affected. They key is to distil the key rationale and allow the others some of the space, but keeping the main impact intact. *If at all possible, avoid holding important conversations with only one of the parties involved.*

Some years ago a young architect colleague did some drafting for a designer working on a West End musical. A great deal of this musical was constructed out of steel frames attached to remotely-controlled truck systems. My colleague was amazed to find that only a few days after having completed the drawing, the completed article itself was being delivered to the theatre. I remember her saying that in the building industry this would have taken several months. It is, then, the immediacy of theatre work which sets it apart from many other forms of activity. Not only that, but it is the understanding of the required response which enables some to succeed in the industry and the lack of it which makes life more difficult for others. We rely on each other to interpret the unspoken.

Questions for Designers and thoughts in the head.
- Is there anything over and above what we see here? *i.e. in the model*
- Does anything move? *In sight? – from where to where?*
- How often? *Implication re drive guidance systems and* **money!**
- How does 'X' enter/exit? *(knowledge of play required, Tosca leaps off the castle ramparts etc.)*
- How truly do we follow the model? *To what extent is this simply indicative?*
- Which bits are practical? *I see a lot of drapes and windows.*
- What is most important to you? *What do we keep getting back to?*
- Have you done a section? *I've got one of the theatre right here.*

Questions for yourself upon seeing a model for the first time:
- Does what you see induce any 'gut' feeling?
- If so, what? e.g. – nothing we haven't done before, or expensive.
- Does the designer appear to have thought it all through?
- Is there development work still to be done?
- Does the ground plan look feasible?
- Does the designer appear to have *idées fixes*?
- Does anything trigger alarm bells? e.g. has the designer not thought through the implications of the rake, or is there anywhere for the offstage chorus?

With lighting design, I have to declare an interest. I have lit many, many shows in many circumstances and in my years 'before the mast' I was an electrical dayman. This is not to say one has some kind of 'soft spot' for lighting designers, but it does say that that experience – before, during and after Production Management experience – provides a good idea as to where they are coming from, so to speak.

Elsewhere in Critical Path Analysis we talk of the lighting designer as being the *one* who has to think and create on his feet, with lots of folk probably standing about. The LD in me wants to get things organised so that the various process of my work can be got through efficiently and without the hassle of competing work from other departments. What I'm seeking is leaving some time for 'tweaking' and finessing. I will use Production Management logic when discussing the immediate next phase of the production process, giving irrefutable reasons why my proposal is undoubtedly the only one worth following. In this, too, is another factor mentioned elsewhere – well-being. The early years taught that there are some things we can do well enough when tired – getting to grips with the potential of a rig is not one of them. Also, the LD often has a really close relationship with his crew. Their welfare will bear on to the LD's capacity as well. The worst cases occur when the electrics team have a raft of building-based tasks – like tending the boilers – which 'just have' to be done. This can be a real irritant. The Production Manager should relieve the situation as far as possible

But, in a more detached sense, the Production Manager and the lighting designer have more in common with each other than the Production Manager and designers in other disciplines. What they both do bears directly on the staff. Both of them will be better regarded by getting this factor right. There is a penalty for getting it wrong.

The LD has for years been the one who invades the auditorium. The LD wants to occupy space which might just be used for seating and making money. So the start of the relationship is to get a mutual understanding of the larger picture.

Q: Are the FOH positions OK for your needs?
Q: If not, where else do you need to be?
(Does this raise other issues: lost seats (money!) safety, licence, power supply?)

It must be obvious that these are far reaching decisions that need to be dealt with very early on indeed, especially if third parties (of any authority) need to become involved. It can't be unreasonable either for an LD to over-bid a bit – after all, at an early stage there are a lot of other ideas flying around as well.

Usually this is not a problem area, but it has to be the Production Manager's responsibility to raise the issue, even just to have it put to one side immediately. This leaves the Production Manager in a better position should minds start to change later . . .

The lighting designer has an interest in the available power supply and the stage lighting installation generally. The Production Manager will want to know how well this accommodates the lighting designer's ideas. The issue is time; time spent rigging and supplying different lighting positions will be greater than time spent installing on to what is 'given'.

At this point, we should bring in the sound designer as well. He and the lighting designer share quite a lot. Both of them, effectively, design arrangements of manufactured articles. The sound man has the slight advantage, insofar that sound effects, recorded music, etc. can be heard beforehand. Their issues now are spatial.

Consider the performance area as a volume into which the designers all put their realised ideas. The needs of all need to be taken on board – the needs of space, separation, lack of interference, etc. The LD needs to be in a specific relationship with the scenery he has to light: the sound designer needs to see clear pathways *to* his microphones and *from* his speakers.

It becomes important, then, not to fix locations until all factors have been visited. The Production Manager's job can be at its most difficult here. He has to be understanding to all and yet prepared to broker compromises in order to move forward.

Whilst the sound designer is in the loop, it should be remembered that sound is increasingly likely to want to reconfigure auditorium arrangements to accommodate live mixing positions, etc. There are, of course, designers of costumes and hats as well. In many cases, perhaps because the basic questions for light and sound designers are the same, the basic wisdom – find out more than you need to know – remains the same for the Production Manager. Most of all, aim to enjoy working together.

Over the years a basic methodology evolved through which the various different strands could be woven together. As with all good managing it begins in the mind.

In my mind I keep a section of a theatre. I can sit in any row and look at the stage. As I move around the seating, the sightlines in my head follow new paths. When inspecting any new proposal one automatically does this. We mustn't forget that the designers, working on models, often tend to sit at a table so they see the set as if from the Dress Circle. I developed the habit, using an adjustable drawing board, of raising it high and sitting in front of models at a higher level than I was. Here I was sitting in the first row of the stalls, usually the worst possible sightlines. This triggered all kinds of debates about lateral and vertical masking, as well as what one was supposed to see through windows, doors or whatever.

These debates usually involve lighting people as well, who will want to hang bars or place booms in and around the set. This is where instinctive geometry comes in. The implications of anything being moved will bear on other things around it. We must know what these implications are. One has to have confidence in one's own judgement. When sitting down to draw, it is not to find out if it will work, but to formalise what has been decided already in the mind.

The ground plan basically tells the staff where to put the scenery in relation to the building or the venue. I learned very early on to ignore such phrases as 'setting line' or 'first available bar' and instead to concentrate on the actual building itself. If, for instance, the plan is for a new production in a regional producing theatre, designed by someone who is experienced with this theatre and the director, it is reasonable to assume that the designer will have designed their work to fit the circumstances. On the other hand, some productions are begun without being certain where they may end up. Or, in some cases, it may be that the designer is remote; he or she might even be abroad, and the knowledge of the specific theatre and the dynamic of its auditorium may not be fully developed. The Production Manager should have an understanding of the spatial relationship and the audience dynamic, so that scenery can be arrayed on the stage so as to give the actors the best possible access to those parts of the stage which offer the best impact. This is the 'point of command' where the actor feels he can most comfortably address the whole audience. It can only really be found by standing in the space and moving about until you find it! This should inform the placing of the scenery within the space.

This is where the ability to think in three dimensions becomes such a useful tool to the Production Manager. Knowing that as things move through a vertical plane, the impact on the various tiers of the auditorium will be different. So, the Production Manager drawing a plan can take these into account. It can be more difficult when the production is still in rehearsal and being evolved, when there may well be things developing through the process which might have an effect on the way the scenery is placed in the theatre.

In recent years it has become much more common to work with computer aided design systems. The ease with which multiple lines can appear on CAD drawings should not mask the fact that what the Production Manager wants from a designer is 'essential' information and not 'non-essential' information. A senior and much respected colleague recently divested himself of the view that there was no point in starting a drawing if you haven't had an idea. Quite often, if a drawing is being done manually, the draughtsman will unwittingly provide the cardinal pieces of information and perhaps omit some of the less important pieces of information which can be taken, effectively, as read.

In a conventional theatre with some approximation of a hanging or flying system, it is received wisdom that the design needs to be reduced to a hanging plot, i.e. all the items in the performance are designated to a specific element of the flying system. This can sometimes mean that when lowered into their correct positions, the rest of the setting follows automatically.

We talked above about looking at a setting with regard to masking. This is an important field because if productions tour, they will often be performed in venues to which they are not specifically suited, i.e. either too big or too small. If the venues are too big, then obviously masking around the set will need to be done in such a way that the setting does not appear to be too far out of space; if the venue is too small, some judicious editing of scenery may have to be undertaken in order for it to fit at all. This is where the Production Manager's basic technical knowledge of theatre will come into play. Remember that in many instances it is the Production Manager who designs the masking, i.e. the designer often produces the set and sets the setting as far as scenery is concerned, and leaves what goes on outside or around it to the Production Management team.

The aim always has to be to best serve the needs of the design by taking the 'raw material' from the designer's information and converting it into full scale reality. Success is measured by the smile on the designer's face when they first see the finished product onstage.

Love's Labours Lost . . . Out of Sight

Laurence Olivier directed *Love's Labours Lost* at the National Theatre (when it was at the Old Vic). One of the key scenes in the play is where Berowne climbed a tree to eavesdrop on his colleague's thoughts about love. The tree was effectively a branch which stuck out at an angle over the acting area, from where Jeremy Brett (Berowne) could direct his asides at the audience. After some time, the production was required to tour. I designed a free-standing unit which would support the tree and the weight of Mr Brett. It could therefore be set wherever suitable in any touring venue.

A lot of the provincial No 1 venues bear very little relationship to the stage space at the Old Vic. I was very worried on one occasion because the sightlines were such that the branch and its attendant support unit had to be placed so far onstage for Mr Brett to be seen, that there was hardly any acting space left in the middle. I took the matter to the highest authority. Sir Laurence immediately suggested that I planned to have the offending item much further off stage, leaving adequate space for the actors in the middle. I did point out that of course Mr Brett would not be clearly visible to many people in the audience. Sir Laurence dismissed my concerns with the following edifying thought: "In 1946, when I did Richard III at the Old Vic, I spent a lot of the first soliloquy standing by the OP Prosc. I then became known as Sir Laurence (f..k the side seats) Olivier."

3 PRODUCTION MANAGERS AND TECHNICAL CREWS

This is one of the most important relationships that the Production Manager has to cultivate. It is the one which, if ill addressed, can cause the most grief. It will be the shortest Chapter in this book. It is served by one cautionary illustration.

By the time I first became a Production Manager I had already worked on the stage and electrics crews in a No1 Touring House, been the technical ASM in a flagship Rep, worked as a stage and electrics dayman and then became a Property Master in the West End and been a Property Master for the National Theatre. I had seen all manner of Production Managers and people doing that kind of thing. I had a very clear idea of what gained a crew's respect and equally what lost it.

In those days the average runs of West End shows tended to be much shorter and fit ups happened fairly frequently. If a production arrived with a Production Manager brimming with confidence and issuing all manner of instructions without any consultation we would decide to do everything exactly as he asked for it, without question – with a smile, of course. In many cases this led to disaster; things had to be undone and done again differently, schedules got disrupted, additional overtime was incurred and angst levels rose rapidly. The poor Production Manager was caught in the middle between his management who saw things getting late and a crew who had no respect for him. The message is simple: talk it through first. Talk it through taking on board the views of the crew. Make sure the reasoning behind the work plan is clear and agreed.

If this is got right the 'spirit' will be right and things encountered on the way will be met with a positive attitude and a united front.

One could go, on but all the essentials of this relationship are contained in this tale.

4 PRODUCTION MANAGERS AND CONTRACTORS

This section covers two broad categories. We don't always identify the separation, but it does help to separate them in analysis. Part of the process is the dividing up of the various needs into separate work packages and the other part is the work and nature of contracting itself.

Contract Breakdown

Ideally, as soon as a Production Manager sees a model, or gathers the general intentions about the next project or production, he will already be beginning to think about how the various tasks involved can be split up. Certainly those Production Managers working with standing establishments' craftsmen will find this procedure reasonably automatic. But, as often said here, a second look is frequently worthwhile. It is obviously important that all the personnel available should be most usefully engaged – and it often happens that there are areas where departments can tend to overlap, the most obvious being the area between prop makers and scenic artists or painters. Flags, banners, cartouches, curtains and other such objects can just as easily made by either.

The overriding criterion must be to ensure that the workload is spread as evenly as possible amongst the personnel available, and as we move increasingly towards an era of genuine multi-skilling, this should become progressively easier. Multi-skilling also offers the Production Manager a far wider variety of projects which can be undertaken 'in house'.

This is where a broad-ranging overview position needs to be initially established and fleshed out over a series of conversations and meetings so as to ensure that all work will be covered by someone. At the same time, it is important to ensure that no specific contracts are let until the whole framework is in place.

Dividing up the tasks can be an interesting, yet mentally taxing experience. Discussions with the design team need to be at an advanced stage for this to work well. This can be where the talk revolves around "what" something is to be. Only when you have decided what an article is to be made of, can a decision about the maker be made.

This is where the pro-active Production Manager has to develop his own clear idea of how he wants things to be constructed, how they might be assembled and the general procedure to be followed in the installation of the production. All of these will have a bearing on the nature of contracts or separation of labour.

A judgement has to be made about the main materials likely to be used. In addition to visible materials, one must be aware of other materials required, such as fixing systems, nails, screws, glues, tacks – in other words, the various methods by which the raw materials can be pulled or fixed into the shapes required. Some knowledge here of paints and solvents is also helpful, so that the Production Manager may take a useful part in conversations about both the decoration of the work and the construction details.

This kind of knowledge comes fairly easily if one has been involved in the construction of scenery or scenic effects. If you come from a another discipline, it would have to be acquired through a different kind of learning process, and a learning-by-rote system at that. I do not believe a Production Manager can function without a good working knowledge of the available raw materials and suppliers. In cases where he is dealing with a raw material which is brand new, some research ability to identify a supplier and manufacturer for something which has never been used in a theatrical context before is essential. This is pivotal to the way theatre develops. The profession has always been quick to utilise, frequently with great innovation, advances which were originally intended for use elsewhere.

One must also be aware of the flammability, durability and 'tourability' of materials. Naturally, different choices would be made in terms of material if one is dealing with a production which is going to remain static on a rep. stage, or within the West End, or built for working in repertoire or touring. In the latter instances we may find we have to use materials which are of a higher grade or finish or easily handled or loaded – or less liable to chip, bend or break. Also relevant Statutory Codes should always be available.

What we are endeavouring to achieve is a situation where we can feel confident that all the work involved is going to happen with the minimum of fuss and disruption. Production Management will know, especially if they have any experience, the capacities of various contractors. Capacity here can mean either volume or range of available expertise, and we must also remember that, to some degree, contractors are like territorial animals. They are most happy when dealing with what they are best at, and are less happy dealing with things which are outside their normal remit. It is, then, important to sense if what is being asked is pushing a contractor into an area of concern. I have known contractors argue towards increasing the amount or style of work which they are good at, at the expense of a Production Manager's better judgement. The worst case in memory was where a contractor produced an armature in wood which had been asked for in metal – only to find that it didn't match the specification. What followed was the necessity of having to make steelwork to support the woodwork – at a greatly increased cost. When the contractor was asked why he had varied the instruction, he could only answer that he made more money producing things in wood!

In the business of dividing up the work between various different subcontractors, one enters into a process of negotiating with one or the other for various different parts and comparing their various prices. In one particular case, it was quite expected that a certain contractor would be engaged to do a rather large tranche of the work. Other contractors, perhaps less experienced ones, had put forward proposals and budgets. When the quote from the expected contractor appeared to be rather large, one had to point out to him that while one would be very happy to see him do the work, his current quote was not competitive. His reply was that if you went below the existing figure, there would be no profit. The relative circumstances at the time meant that this contractor would not get the work. Of course, an analysis can always be that he put the price up because he didn't want the job in the first place! The smaller concerns managed to do the work very well!

Having got the broad outlines clarified, the next job is to define the boundaries, or interfaces, between the different areas of contract and work. This may involve the odd bit of cajoling in order to make sure there are no leaks or 'gaps between stools' through which the unforeseen can pass.

This, too, falls into two broad areas. First, where contractor A has to fabricate something to a point which then gets passed on to contractor B, it must be absolutely clear as to the condition expected by contractor B when he receives the work. Contractor A must be made aware of contractor B's requirements and understand and agree that he can satisfy them. Contractor B must also agree that he will maintain contact with contractor A during the procedure and at any time required furnish contractor A with details of any additional requirements. Into such an arrangement would fall items such as state of surfaces, pre-drilled holes, means of lifting, maximum weight to be carried, overall size and dimension, safe handling instructions, assembly procedures, etc. The second style of interface normally comes when the installation is being carried out. Here, one is more concerned that those in charge of flying a piece know whether or not they have to provide the fittings and attachments between the article and the flying system or whether they are the responsibility of the fabricator. The fabricator will require to know whether he is responsible for determining the number and dimensions of supports and their correct labelling.

Matters become more complex in the electronic area. Here, it is possible that components may arrive from different manufacturers. It is important, then, that they all know which style of connector is to be applied between the various different components. Equally, they must know who is to provide the connection between one piece of equipment and another.

It must also be made clear that part of the contractor's responsibility must be to ensure that his work does not interfere with the work of others. This may involve liaison over the use of access equipment, clearing debris, power supply, earthing, manuals, etc. to assist the work of others.

It is not unreasonable for the Production Manager to want to hear of the contractors liaising, but it is advisable that the Production Manager should want to see a manifestation that this is actually taking place. Too often one hears contractors say "we worked successfully together before", or "we've always managed as a team". Given the fact that the pressures on any contractor are always going to vary, you cannot be certain that the circumstances which have successfully worked in the past are necessarily mirrored by those which exist in the current project.

Another area which needs to be considered in the separation of the work into the various contract areas is the Production Manager's view as to the nature and shape of the installation or production process. It is important that the Production Manager develops a view, with the help of the contractors' opinions, as to the progress on a daily/weekly basis of the installation, e.g. where do you expect to be at the end of Day 1? If we haven't developed this scenario, then we are unable to answer the question, 'how are we doing?' In extreme cases it may be desirable to ask the contractor whether he would agree to a time-scale being written into a contract. Even if it is not written into a contract, a time-scale must be consistently borne in mind, and, as noted above, contractors whose work starts to impinge on another's ability to complete, will begin to find themselves running into a breach of agreement.

This whole process is quite delicate and can only be improved by analysing how one approaches on successive occasions. After all, each production is different and the answers cannot always be the same. This is where the Production Manager's ability to analyse becomes so important.

The gist of this must be that the Production Manager should feel confident that all the contractors are doing something which they are equipped and skilled to do and have adequate time to complete their work before the relevant articles are needed.

The Contract

It is my belief that in the UK too few people take enough notice of Contract in terms of production. Contract means the existence of an agreed and written understanding between a supplier and a company. 'Agreed understanding' means that someone agrees to undertake to produce something for the theatre to a certain given standard and by a certain given date. This is of sufficient importance to warrant considerable discussion. It is an essential part of a Production Manager's required knowledge, especially where the management aspect is concerned.

The starting point is perhaps the performance itself. The ticket sold represents a contract to provide the performance to the purchaser. Failure to present the performance will necessitate the return of the money and maybe more. So, as a Production Manager prepares for a new show, he is aware that if any of the arrangements he has made don't work properly his employers could well be unable to fulfill their own obligations. Sometimes it may well be beneficial to remind suppliers and contractors of their involvement in this complex chain of responsibility.

Many countries have in place consumer protection legislation, so if one buys everyday articles off the shelf, there is an expectation that it will do certain things. Nevertheless, we should always check that we have what we wanted. Perhaps not going so far as to count every screw in the box, but certainly to check that they are of the right size! The law will maintain your right to have what you purchased as generally understood or stated by the supplier, and the sale document effectively forms the contract. Second hand dealers, not just in cars, who specialise in any field are not exempt from the law. The law considers that their expertise should tell them whether an article is fit to be sold and function properly. They have to take back goods and refund if the purchaser can prove that the purchased object doesn't do what it is supposed to do.

The more complex contracts arise when specialist manufactured items are being acquired. Presumably they are being bought because their specification satisfies the use they are to be put to, and this is usually written down by the manufacturer. It is my view that something more than a simple invoice and receipt is required; the dealer or manufacturer should acknowledge that what they are selling will perform to the given criteria. Durability and longevity need to be taken into account as well. This will satisfy most of those things that come in boxes that are destined for semi-portable lives, like luminaires or loud-speakers which are due to be handled and used by personnel trained in their use. If the equipment is of a new design or layout, the supplier should contractually agree to provide operational training to specified personnel – within the contract price.

A change occurs again when something requires 'installation'. This category includes installed dimmers and permanently wired sound components. A problem here is that some manufacturers seem to want to leave this vital aspect to others. If subsequently things don't perform to the spec, one finds the installer and the manufacturer both blaming the other and the poor purchaser none the better off. If there is any choice, the manufacturer who is prepared to install should be used. There can be no avoiding of responsibility. The devices can be tested and handed over directly. If the maker is not present, who then is supposed to perform tests?

The other danger in using separate installers is that they may well have other pressures which will impinge on the quality of their work. During the 'lottery boom' of the late 1990s a number of horror stories came out where poor installation practices were likely to have a detrimental effect on the long term performance of the equipment. Luckily some were spotted but the likelihood is that some installations were not given a thorough enough check before being accepted.

When an installation is being planned, the parameters of the work need to be defined and embodied in the contract between the supplier and the purchaser. These should include: start date and time, items such as access equipment, lifting gear, power supply or labour that the purchaser should provide for the supplier. It is important that the supplier installer/supplier agrees that this list of requirements is full and complete. It is not unknown for the wiser supplier to go a bit over the top here but if the result is a trouble free installation delivered on time, then its probably worth it. This can only be decided following a fairly exhaustive dialogue.

Check everything!

Is a parking permit needed, will the crew need transport, rest or washing facilities, etc.? It is then important that those responsible for receiving the equipment, a) know what they have to get ready, and, b) that it is part of the contract. It is, depending on the magnitude, imperative to have a 'presence' when the work is due to start – if not the Production Manager, then one of his staff. If for any reason work doesn't start on time, then immediately one must ask what the knock-on effect is likely to be. In most cases the first enquiry of this nature will elicit an "it'll be alright" kind of answer. The situation now needs monitoring fairly carefully. This can be the least pleasant part of the work because the contractor will be not too happy about admitting that there is a problem. This is where painstaking preparation is highly beneficial. First and foremost one wants work done on time. Of course, one can get the contractor to agree that all that was required was present and seek to identify the cause of the time problem. Once identified it may be possible to help. The one thing you can't give is more time. Longer working hours or extra personnel may solve the problem.

The last of the purchase categories is where we buy something that has to be built in or assembled on site, such as a flying system or orchestra lift. This usually means time and the maker's staff being on site. The conditions need to be carefully considered. It is not in anyone's interest to have an installation delayed or running late. Try to establish just how much ancillary space around the work area will be needed and ensure that others keep out of the way during the installation process.

When drawing up a set of purchase orders, installations and contracts, make sure that all concerned know of each others' existence. Not only that, but where any kind of interface, physical or electronic, occurs then the parties must undertake that what you want is a 'working system' and that *nobody will be paid until the entire system including the work of different companies is proven to work effectively*. This provides a situation where a no surprise scenario is the result.

Given the need for a complete working system, it is important that all concerned understand fully what the whole system has to do, and their roles within it. The role of any one contributor is subservient to the whole. This is where management skills are called upon. Meetings between all are much more useful than one-to-one's with individual companies. A good approach is to refer always to the whole, and subsequently to what each contributor brings to it. This cements the notion that we are all in the same boat and that success will be evenly applauded. Remember that manufacturers and suppliers need to sell their wares and nowadays employ sophisticated sales skills to convince you that their particular product is the best. Don't allow them to succeed in this type of approach. When the decision is taken to use a certain company it should be approached along the lines of "We think that your contribution, as discussed, will fit well with other companies we are approaching. Do you have any problem working with any of them?" Don't let them think that they are included because of their superior product – more because they can interface successfully with the others to the common end.

Questions

Selecting suppliers and contractors is a key part of the Production Manager's work. The longer one does it, the less likely it will be that all the firms approached will be totally unknown. Nevertheless, in the back of the mind some of the following parameters should be present:

- Does the required work fall within the normal expertise of the company?
- Does the company 'need' the work?
- Will the work be considered 'big' in the context of the company's business profile?
- Does the person taking the instructions have a clear understanding of what is required?
- Does the person taking instructions directly relate to the people actually carrying out the work?
- Do they have time to do the work?
- Are they solvent?
- Do they publish accounts?
- Will they sign a contract?
- Do they usually come in on budget?

Questions to ask contractors:
- Do you comprehend what is required?
- Can you provide the service - product?
- Can you provide it within the required time frame?
- Are you prepared to sign a contract?
- Are you *empowered* to sign a contract?
- To whom do *you* report?
- Does your company take legal advice?
- Are directors shareholders?

- Have you read the draft contract?
- Do you acknowledge the implications?
- Is your price agreed by your senior people?

The next step is to select the appropriate clauses which need to be in any contract. There are two over-arching points we need to be clear about. Firstly, contracts should indicate which countries' law applies and, secondly, when dealing with a foreign language, no matter what language meetings are conducted in, all written communications emerging from your own office should be in your own language. Equally, foreign colleagues may write to you in their own language. The burden of translation is with the recipient.

Contract Pro Forma

The contract should clearly state:
- The parties to the contract.
- Their legal addresses and/or styles, e.g. limited company, company limited by guarantee, sole trader, registered charity, etc.
- The scope of the work (annexe a schedule of work to be done).
- Time is of the essence.
- Date for completion.
- Date for delivery.
- Responsibility for delivery.
- Penalties for lateness.
- Definitions of all acronyms.
- Ownership of the work, e.g. point of hand-over, or acceptance without liens.
- Insurance responsibilities in respect of employer liability, personal liability, property damage, consequential loss, full replacement and replacement of collateral damage to the work of others.
- Complete working system includes work of others.
- Contract fee, payment schedule and conditions.
- Scope of design information to be supplied to contractor.
- Confidentiality in respect of design information.
- Design information is the property of the producing management.
- That the contractor remains responsible for any sub-contracts they let. (No such contracts without prior approval.)
- Schedule of support to be supplied by producing management.

- The contractor will supply the management with all warranties, where applicable, for components in contractor's work in the management's name.
- The contractor will demonstrate that his work complies with the agreed specifications before final handover.
- The management and its representatives have the right to inspect the ongoing work at the contractor's premises.
- The contractor will, upon completion, supply the management with "as built" drawings which can include wiring diagrams, connector pin layouts, flow charts, engineering calculations, software identity, etc.
- The contractor will provide training for management personnel within the frame of the contract.
- The contractor will ensure that all instructions conform to safe working practices. Risk assessment documentation will be available where management personnel are to operate or handle the contractor's work.
- The contractor will attend production meetings and report on progress.
- The contractor will accept all responsibilities for his personnel during the course of the work.
- The contractor will integrate the work of others into a complete working system.
- The contractor will work on management premises to schedules prepared by the management.
- Arbitration procedures.
- The national basis of law of the contract. e.g. 'The law of England will apply'.
- This list is not exhaustive!

NB: Re: Consequential Loss Insurance:

If a lorry carrying scenery slides off the road in a snowstorm, two types of liability are present:
   (1) The repair/replacement of damaged components in the load.
   (2) The loss of income due to the late or non-arrival of the scenery at the destination venue leading to cancelled performances.
The latter represents a consequential loss.

A contract pro forma can be printed off as required. Go through it with prospective suppliers. Clauses can be deleted if irrelevant. Don't sow the seeds of discontent by deleting clauses which protect your product.

Re: Warranties.

When bespoke engineering is made for a production, it will normally include off-the-peg items like motors, gearboxes, clutches, etc. They will carry manufacturers' warranties. Although the engineer will buy in the first instance, he is not the end user. The warranty should indicate the end user. Should a component fail, the Production Manager can go direct to the manufacturer. This bears more specifically on longer running shows, some of which have outlived their builders!

On any project which involves touring, or sequential moves from place to place etc., it is always worthwhile to build in break points in the contractual arrangements. Thus, if for any reason at all the project has to be delayed, postponed or put off, it is possible to withdraw from the existing arrangements with transporters, installers, insurers, etc. with the minimum of disruption and financial burden.

Technology Can Go Too Far

Some time in the 1990s the London Ambulance Service installed, with some fanfare, a new system for allocation and dispatch. The idea was that the vehicle nearest the casualty be sent to attend. It was going to be more efficient, reduce waiting times, etc. Well it didn't work. After a couple of days of unmitigated chaos the Ambulance Service reverted to the old system and carried on as before. The millions of pounds spent on new technology having been to no avail. One absorbed the flurry in the media about how all the new high tech kit hadn't quite come up to scratch. As a Production Manager one felt that the very least reaction was a letter to a paper. It was written and printed in the *Independent* newspaper.

The letter contained two strands: firstly that we should question who was letting the contracts on behalf of the Ambulance Service and what experience did they have of this kind of work? Certainly one would not have expected the indigenous staff to have anything like the required level of expertise. The thought of millions of pounds of public money being spent via inexperienced personnel in thrall to experienced smooth talking salesmen did occur.

Secondly, and more pertinent to the theatre, was the question as to how much of the complex arrangement of computers and related sending, receiving, amplifying, locating and message relaying equipment with in the whole system was 'new'? It's a Production Manager's nightmare. If everything is new then its always going to be more difficult to track faults through the system. Equipment which has a track record does bring with it the balance of probabilities. You know better where you are. Because we, in the theatre, have to put such great store in reliability one cannot recommend wholesale embracing of new technology. Make sure a few old friends are in the package somewhere. After all, all systems are composed of many, many parts. The only advice can be that the devil you know can help with the gods of innovation. When this was being written the London Ambulance service had still not successfully integrated the proposed wonder system.

The lesson has always got to be to go for the simplest fail-safe option if there is one. If there is not, see if one can be found. A memorable case was that of a life-size figure which had to sway. Complicated solutions were coming forward involving bearings for the base. Then the lateral thinker came up with simplicity itself. The figure had a metal armature. He acquired about 700 mm of good old steel drain-pipe, quite thick, and fixed the feet of the statue to the pipe. The figure rocked from side to side on the pipe with no bearing at all, its own weight holding it down, but just to make sure we nailed a couple of bits of wood to the floor either side . . . .

5 PRODUCTION MANAGER AND PERFORMANCE

Production Management work is geared to performances – something simply stated, perhaps, but it needs to be kept in mind. It is not about models on display or framed costume drawings or any other permanent artefact. I once saw a model of a set I had production managed in an exhibition. Twenty or more years had lapsed and the model, by itself, looked lovely but without the trappings of a live performance and the excitement of preparation and creation, it had a curiously detached quality. It had lost its purpose and become an artwork.

I think it is important that Production Managers have some background of performance work. Without being disrespectful it is often the case that designers, because of different disciplines and increasing specialisation in their training, don't all have a well of useful backstage experience to draw upon. There is a discernable difference between a show which runs easily and one which the crew find awkward or problem prone. I'm also sure that positive vibes permeate through to the cast, enhancing their work as well – and the reverse, of course.

Nothing is accidental. Everything that happens is as a result of some decision being taken somewhere by someone. It is our job to plan towards trouble free performances. It's not just a question of machinery, but of the dynamic. It's those awkward moments when some massive object has to be set in semi-darkness or loads of darkly-clad people have to scurry about in the gloom changing the furniture settings that need avoiding. Many times one has heard a disgruntled crew member wondering which ****ing person planned this in the first place.

The only way to get a real grip on this situation is from the very first meetings or study of early models. We have to put ourselves in the place of the crew and see it from their point of view. This is where our first-hand experience comes in. This, too, is where the designers, especially those who lack backstage experience, may not fully understand one's thinking. Many directors understand that any evidence of clumsiness will act to the detriment of the whole production. The powers of reason need to be trotted out. Scenarios drawn whereby the outcome of pursuing the project as first foreseen, may not be as good as a more practical, less risky approach.

In the planning stage, there are also key issues to do with running costs to be addressed. The prime factor will usually be labour costs, i.e. the cost of crewing the show. There will be some inevitable base costs of stage management and of course the cast, but from there on there can be different approaches.

To make the point, let's look at the two extremes. Firstly, a theatre with a large standing crew bears no particular additional cost if they are required to 'work' the show. This means that the PM can plan for them to move trucks, operate winches, strike rostra, and so on.

The other extreme could be a commercial production expecting a long run. Here, developments in remote control technology have become a financially sensible option. Luckily, the more these techniques are used, the greater the developed expertise becomes. Thus one operator sitting at a console can operate a variety of moving pieces to a pre-programmed plan.

Most situations will fall somewhere between the two extremes. So what criteria should we be using to help ourselves? Fail-safe has got to be the answer. We want something essentially simple which works well without the involvement of chance. Moving 'traditional' scenery is a time-worn skill and is a coefficient of time and numbers. Winches have been used for centuries as well for driving items along tracks, either hung above or in slots in the stage floor. The application of powered rather than manual drive to stage machinery, moving both vertically and horizontally, is now readily available.

Let us look again at fail-safe. If the production is a play in three acts with set changes behind the tabs then there is less to concern us. We have to put an adequate number of staff on duty with whatever lifting or moving devices they need to do the change safely.

The productions where sets move in view are a different matter. What are we looking for? A smooth controlled movement from A to B or a sudden crash or happening? Are we *supposed* to see it? Is the movement of whatever is involved part of the visual dynamic or is it part of a means of getting from one configuration to another? Does it happen frequently? The answers to these questions will point the way to deciding the best approach to the decision. Here is a simple example. A play in the West End had a short scene played on a truck downstage centre at the opening of the second Act. At the end of the scene the truck had to disappear in a blackout. Other than a couple of fly cues it was the only scenic movement in the play. It was decided to use fixed lateral castors on the truck. A wire from the truck lay along the stage running to the prompt corner where the offstage end was tied off to a ring plate screwed into the stage floor. On the blackout a manual cue was given and a crew member wearing industrial gloves picked up the wire. Because the offstage end was fixed the only thing that could move was the truck. The act of picking up the wire overcame the inertia of the truck and the crewman had no difficulty in simply pulling the truck into the wings hand over hand where he stopped it with his boot. It could not have been simpler and it did all that was needed for the play being preset behind tabs. However, as we know, fixed castors are only as good as the surface they are rolling on and tend to meander. Therefore if this truck had required multiple movements each successive one would have left the truck on a slightly different angle. To guarantee the positioning some sort of guidance slot or track would be needed. This would bring with it a degree of friction and increase the work load of the offstage puller. As his job gets more difficult the likelihood of error creeps in so a mechanical drive of some sort will become necessary.

Using this as an example, always look for the simplest way of doing something; only be persuaded towards more complex solutions when the simple starts to lose its fail-safe aspect. When the plate has to fall off the shelf the prop man, on cue, gives it a little prod from behind with a stick. We could probably arrange an electronic trigger – but is it really worth it?

This book is not about stage engineering as such. Our engineers can produce the most wonderful things. As Production Managers we have to look beyond and select what is best for us in the circumstances we face. Always come back to the performance and ask whether the options under discussion will work time and time again with minimal maintenance. Will parts wear out and need replacing? Again, always remember that the more parts there are, the greater the possibility of malfunction. Whatever is decided should not leave one thinking "I hope it works". If it does, then more homework is required. All of this thinking will be put to the test at the Technical Rehearsal.

Technical Rehearsal

The Technical Rehearsal, or 'Tech', is the point in the development of any production at which all the various ingredients and disciplines are put together for the first time. If it is well done, the production will carry on in a smooth and, hopefully, successful way. If the Tech is not undertaken in the right spirit, confusion and depression may frequently be the result.

The material ingredients involved are: set, props, costumes, lighting and the sound system. We also have to understand that some ingredients arrive as a result of functions that have already taken place. The sound effects must be developed by going through the sounds in the auditorium space and setting the sound levels, roughly perhaps, so that the operator has a workable plot against which to operate in the first instance. Similarly, a lighting rig, having been installed, focused and then committed to a plotting or lighting session, becomes a completed ingredient.

The acting/performing company is also an ingredient, albeit non-hardware. If the acting company comes to the theatre badly rehearsed, or unrehearsed, not knowing where they should come in from or on what chair they are to sit, etc, then the ingredient has not been well formed and is just as likely to impair the quality of the final product as is the late arrival of a costume, sound effect, or whatever. The importance of the fact that the rehearsal process is a preparation for the company to go on stage cannot be over stressed. When confronted with the reality of the stage, there should be no surprises *(see also Critical Path Analysis, Chapter 7)*.

Therefore, for a proper/technical rehearsal to take place, the Production Management must clarify that all of the constituent ingredients are ready – the point being that, if you attempt to do a technical rehearsal without one of the ingredients, you may well have to repeat the whole exercise for the benefit of that ingredient when it eventually does arrive. This is time-consuming and demoralising and, in the professional theatre, expensive.

The technical rehearsal takes place so that we can make adjustments to the ingredients to help them blend together. It is a time for creative activity by everybody concerned. The fact that things may get altered does not mean that they were initially badly conceived; it means that with the addition of other factors which were not present when light plotting, for instance, was taking place, a change may have to be made. This is quite reasonable. If the Tech has been well done, then the next full stage rehearsal will be a successful, non-stopping dress rehearsal. If a dress rehearsal has to be stopped for a technical reason, then it implies that the Tech rehearsal has not been properly conducted.

Preparing for the Tech involves making sure that all the working personnel, including the company, know where they should be at the beginning and are fully prepared, costumed, with all their relevant information, ready to start the process. It is important that all technical and stage management make themselves comfy in their work stations and that they can see what they need to see or be at ease during long waits where matters relevant to others are being resolved. The main thing is that staff stay in place and ready should they be asked. A surreptitious light and a racing newspaper should perhaps be given a blind eye. It is also sensible to start at a time when everybody is reasonably fresh. If one department is nearing the end of a long work period, then they will tire sooner, or at worst have to break, leaving the process high and dry.

The last part of the preparation process is to establish what can be called 'performance conditions'. These are the lighting, sound, set and other factors that pertain to each department at the beginning of the performance. By this time, the DSM (the person giving the cues) should have determined the opening sequence, i.e. which department or individual gets the very first cue from which all other activity will follow. Having received clearance from the stage manager to start, that cue is given and the opening begins. As a general rule, where there are long sequences of activity, it is best to let them work their way through, even if things go wrong, so that a full review can be taken at the end.

Good stage management is vital to the whole process. It is essential that communication be straight and simple between director and stage management. It is the stage management who interpret the director's wishes into cue information that can be operated by the technical personnel. The Production Manager's role here can be the extra, more technical eyes in the house, available to offer alternatives or assistance where needed. No one should know better than the Production Manager the capacities of the technical departments.

When something is not right, the technical rehearsal has to be stopped. It should be stoppable by *anybody* who sees a problem. There is absolutely no point going into a function or sequence if you know full well that it is not going to work, so it is my belief that anybody in the entire company has a perfect right to say: "Stop, I have a problem." There is also lurking danger in going ahead and nothing accidentally going wrong – *it will go wrong when you don't want it to*. This is the critical point of running a technical rehearsal, i.e. analysing what the problem is and dealing with it as quickly as possible. Doing this requires a clear understanding of under whose responsibility each problem resides (i.e. if it is to do with the company, it could well be the director, but if it is to do with the set, it is the designer who must resolve the issue). The

Production Manager has a prime role here. Sometimes when the creative adrenalin flows, new ideas arrive. The Production Manager may have to say, "It wasn't designed or built to do that" or "It will take x hours to make the required changes", or "I have no budget left!". On the other hand, he should try to say, "Great, we'll give it a go".

For cues being operated by technical personnel, there are only a limited number of things that can actually be wrong. Cues can either be too early, too late, too fast, too slow, or simply the wrong article presented. Gone are the days of "The lights don't look right". Therefore, as soon as someone says "Stop", it is up to the stage management to say "Why have we stopped? What is the problem?" and then define it in the above terms, suggest an alteration to the plot and re-set so that the sequence be run again.

This brings us to the issue of re-starting. It is always best to take the advice of the person giving the cues as to the most appropriate point in the script at which to re-commence running any sequence which has been stopped. This is because this person knows what cues have to be given and will have ascertained the sensible point at which to begin a sequence over again. It should not be a matter of dismay if a sequence has to be run a number of times with detail changes, to ensure that it works to the satisfaction of all the concerned parties.

It must be borne in mind that for the Tech to be successful, there are different agendas for different people. The director wants to see the show looking as it had been conceived, the stage management and staff have the further responsibility of wanting to ensure that what they are proposing to do is likely to be successful and trouble-free on a regular basis, and it may well be that stage management want to recommend changes of detail so as to facilitate trouble-free running in the future.

Every time you stop a technical rehearsal, a certain amount of time is taken to resolve the issue and then get the rehearsal started again. Therefore, it is good to have a view as to some things which *need not stop* a technical rehearsal, but can certainly be taken as a note and dealt with by the relevant department later on.

An example of this might be someone pulling the wrong coloured hankie out of their pocket. This is not the occasion for stopping a rehearsal with all the time involved, but simply writing down 'handkerchief needs to be changed'. On the other hand, stopping to do things which should have been dealt with in rehearsal, for instance, is desperately frustrating, time consuming and counter-productive.

I can remember an actress 'of a certain age' being quite unhappy with the dressing of a bed into which she had to climb decorously, and in this case 45 minutes were taken discussing things which should well have been dealt with earlier had she visited the workshops so that the bed with its bedding could have been on stage in the agreed mode. One sensed the frustration of the company as they saw the minutes ticking by together with their estimates as to when they might be getting home for supper.

On shows where there are many costume changes, it may well be necessary to run parts of the production twice to check that the changes can be done in time. What you do here is run the technical sequence first to ensure that all the lighting and sound cues are working, having instructed the performer(s) *not to do their costume change*, up to the point where the performer re-enters dressed in a new costume. You then stop, go back to the beginning of the sequence, i.e. before the performer leaves for their change, and then run through the sequence again, this time with the performer changing. This should indicate whether or not the performer has adequate time to complete the costume change. It matters less in which order you do these two functions, but they both have to be done to reassure everybody that it is a feasible quick change. Stage Management have to be very careful in their estimation of which may be tight costume changes and be prepared to indicate which chunks need to be re-run, because this information is not going to come from the director; it is entirely driven by the stage management and the costume department.

Having stated at the beginning that it is absolutely essential to have all ingredients present, there are, as ever, times when judgment will lead you to a different answer. There is the issue of money. Expensive things, like bands and orchestras, can be integrated at a later phase when all technical details have been sorted out because it is far too expensive to have these people sitting around doing nothing while you sort out other problems. There may also be very expensive consumable effects which can be subject to changing the plan, e.g. bombs, smoke, etc., or food sequences which are a law unto themselves. Another consideration is safety. Where the cast have to work on mobile scenery, e.g. trucks or revolves, it is obviously sensible to run the first stage rehearsals using stage mechanics in work light, so that the cast become used to the varying positions of the scenic elements before being subjected to the varying light conditions which will apply later.

There are other occasions which will occur when a variation from the usual plan may be acceptable, but it is advised that in all instances you start from the assumption that you get every ingredient together and be argued away from it only by superior logic or *force majeure*.

Technical rehearsals are not necessarily fun, but they are an essential part of the process. They may take a long time, and they may take a lot of patience. It is essential that the stage management keep an idea of the time so that members of the staff can have breaks at reasonable times for refreshment or what are now called 'comfort breaks'. In the case of extremely long technical rehearsals of period plays, suggest that once the costumes have been seen and vetted under light conditions, that the cast may change into more comfortable rehearsing clothes in which to carry on the work. This gives some protection to the clothes and at the same time, keeps the cast comfy. After all, a technical rehearsal can go on for a day or more and it is never likely that a member of the cast will have to wear costume for as long at any other occasion. There is absolutely no point in making the cast uncomfortable at this point in the proceedings, or adding to the wear and tear on the costume. Here, too, the cast may require assistance in a heavy period dress production in simply acquiring the necessities of life, e.g. some refreshments, it being far too lengthy a process to change to go out if a break is only of an hour's duration.

The most desirable outcome of a technical rehearsal is that all departments may well have some notes to deal with or be in a position to start writing parts of their plot in a firmer hand. Then the move to preparing the performance space (stage) for the first dress rehearsal follows naturally.

The Production Manager should want to know in each case, from each deptartment, how long they need to complete these tasks. People will say: "I've just got to . . ." That doesn't tell you anything. What is wanted is a time – in minutes. Make people be specific so you can judge for yourself. Once crew realise that you will not be mollified with half misinformation, the process gets easier and easier. Only then should the Dress Rehearsal call be issued. If the time is pre-ordained, decisions will have to be taken as to how much can reasonably be done now as opposed to later.

To sum up, the smooth running performance must be the final arbiter of the Production Manger's thinking from the first look at design ideas to the point where it is handed over to the stage management for the duration of the run. No matter how well everything has been made or how well all the departments have gelled together – if the running of the show is at all chancy then the job will not have been well done.

A Design Too Far . . .
the Production Manager Overrules

Whilst I was still a drama student, during the last Millennium, I enjoyed the experience of being indentured slave labour at the Bristol Old Vic Theatre for their Christmas production. The production in question was a Julian Slade & Dorothy Reynolds musical (not a pantomime) which, owing to their popularity was scheduled for a 10-week run and, I believe, something like 80% capacity had already been sold by the time the production was to open.

After a rousing opening chorus, the second scene was due to open with Dorothy Reynolds entering through what appeared to be her cottage door to stand in the 'morning sunshine' to discuss matters with the audience.

To effect this, the designer had provided for a large French flat, replete with windows, window boxes, flowers, the door of course, a wall heavily textured with, at the top, suggestions of roofing and guttering. This device was rigged on to the Georgian drum and shaft system by our master flyman, Frank Fresco. Suffice it to say that the weight of the flat and the age of the small pulleys produced such friction that the whole thing moved at what might best be described as 'very creakily'. So, for the first few runs, the gap between the end of the rousing opening chorus and Ms Reynolds' entrance was interminable. Virtually the day before we opened, in the morning, we were reviewing the situation with the stage management and Production Manager. Heads were scratched as to how this awkwardness might be overcome and no sensible answer seemed to be forthcoming.

At this point the Production Manager, after some consideration, simply said: "We'll paint a cloth." Within minutes, a cloth had been ordered from our local suppliers, the French flat was being de-rigged and, before the end of that day and into the evening, the painters were hard at work on painting the cloth which was to supplant the French flat. It should perhaps be noted that the size of the stage at Bristol meant that the cloth was not of massive dimensions.

The significance of this in my memory was that the Production Manager was effectively the only person who could take this decision. He had something to do, he had to override the needs of the designer and no-one else in the assembly had the authority to indent for the expenditure so incurred. Expenditure of course had already been incurred on the French flat which was effectively then junk, and the additional cost of a new cloth plus the time spent to put it in. By the time we reached our final dress rehearsal the following day, all was well and the show proceeded to almost 100% business throughout its 10-week run.

Uneasy Lies The Head That Wears a Crown

Production Managers enjoy developing a good relationship with contractors. These contractors can be builders, painters, prop makers, or whatever, but we all recognise that these relationships, if they are good, ease the path towards successful completion of productions. At the same time it must be remembered that we are unfortunately in what can sometimes be a rather nasty business. In my own recollection is the situation where an excellent scenic artist had produced some excellent work for a production. Unfortunately, for him, he had be sub-contracted by a senior contractor who was suffering enormous cash-flow problems which he had managed to conceal. In order to generate some income, the prime contractor delivered the work of his sub-contractors to the site. However, because the prime contractor was well behind on his own part of the work, the full sums quite obviously were not paid. When the painting firm contacted us to say that they had not been paid and where was their money, etc. Unfortunately one had to say that they weren't owed anything because they were sub-contracted by someone else and that because the prime contractor had not performed his contract, we did not owe them any further money. These things make developing long-term personal relationships very difficult, but in the long run the Production Manager must remember to whom he is primarily responsible.

6 MONEY

Budgeting is not just a question of assessing the amount of material required for a production, together with items bought in from contractors outside, or the amount of man hours to be absorbed in the construction and for final fitting up. It is also a question of being able to distance oneself far enough from the unit in question to ensure that you have not become too absorbed in detail and have lost track of one or more vital items.

ITT one of the biggest, multinational telecommunications companies in the world, divided its interests into several large divisions. Each one was given a set of parameters regarding income, expenditure, profit, etc. When the senior management met to monitor progress and plan ahead, they would look at the results of the divisions in turn. Where the figures matched the parameters, they quickly moved on to the next set of figures. This meant that their full concentration could be put to where the results were for any reason different from the prediction. This works in smaller situations as well. The reduction in stress is worthwhile. It is called a "no surprises" system.

In any production there will always be some fixed costs or 'givens'. It could be labour where the basic wage has been taken into the annual overhead or comes with the rent of the theatre. It could be a maintained stock of materials or it could be free rehearsal space. The first thing is to identify what fits into this bracket. What we want to know is precisely what we have control over and what we don't. If the overheads do cover some of the nominal costs of the production it is sensible to make them work as hard as possible. Equally, *we must know the cut off point*. Production Management is usually seen as the work of getting productions opened. Theoretically, therefore, then no costs incurred after the first night should be set against the PM's budget. This is not always so. One of the crossover areas is consumables where the PM might organise the bulk purchase of smoke pots or confetti cannons and pass them over to the running crew, who will only buy more when the initial supply runs out. The second purchase will be set against the running of the production without question but shouldn't the initial purchase be as well?

The Production Manager must also take into account the needs of the different specialists working towards creating the final production. This is perhaps on the surface an over simplification because one would imagine that most people are aware of what their needs might be. However, I believe that the Production Manager, to be sensible, needs to delve a little deeper – especially where new techniques are being involved.

There are occasions for instance whereby the access equipment in any given theatre is not going to be either adequate of effective when it comes to focusing a lighting rig over a complicated structure set on the stage floor. The job might need some kind of specialised kind of access equipment or some specialised kind of rig to be constructed to enable the focusing to take place. It is not simply a question in this category of ensuring that the carpenter has enough lengths of timber or steel tube to make the scenery, but that everybody has not only the materials they need to use but the tools they need to work it, and that they are not wasting *their* time trying to get hold of these items or trying to work without the correct tools.

In a 'no surprise system', a Production Manager, having been told that a production will have a budget of X thousand pounds should, with the general agreement of the management, be allowed to proceed unilaterally without too much reference upwards, provided that the finished product is going to fall within the budgeted figure. He needs only to alert the management if, for reasons either not of his creation or changing circumstances, the project would appear to be exceeding the budget.

Projected budgeting should tell him if the budget figure is going to be inadequate (see diagram p77). I believe that the management must trust the Production Manager to get the best possible deal for them. His efforts will produce the most cost effective use of the management's money in terms of man hours and materials and finished product on the stage. He too must also trust the management that at his behest the management will make payments to the people when he instructs payment to be made. The latter can be a problem, especially if you are working with a new management which is unknown to suppliers; if payment is not forthcoming the supply of the goods can be held up or even interrupted. It is up to the Production Manager to tell the management quite openly that these are the problems and make them aware that they will have to find ready and available cash to make payments to suppliers as and when he says they should be made. This again is part of the trust that has to exist between the two parties.

Budget Preparation

Areas which commonly produce the same results are a good place to start. i.e. if the costs of lighting usually turn out to be the same within a spread of 10-15% then this would be a reasonable start point. Putting in a figure at the higher end of the spread will give some flexibility. However, this only really works when there are past records to work from.

Above it was noted that one needs to be clear about what one has control of. This is the point where the thinking should come together. Obviously scenery has to be made but that covers materials, labour, contracts, painting, transport and even installation. Remember that the budget is a tool. It is there to help maintain control. So on a larger complex production more columns or lines may be needed. The ideal is to keep the big variables separate. If this is not done then the rogue behaviour of one area may affect another. For this reason I'm not always in favour of standard forms because they can never fit every situation. I can understand why this approach appeals to upper management who want to use the figures for different analyses. Provided the extra information we need can be distilled into the format required by the management there should be no limit to the additional lines we add. The budget first tells us how much we are planning to spend and ideally we should not start spending until all information has been collated into the budget.

So divide and sub divide so that the factors are separated. This has to be an exercise of judgement. When I worked in a small producing house with our own workshops the cost of the 'set' for each play was the cost of the materials bought by the carpenter. All other costs had been taken into the overheads. Even earlier at the Bristol Old Vic we were able, near the end of a season, to go even finer and build shows using second hand timber; however we always bought new canvas for the painters to work on. 'Set' was canvas, glue, tacks, and paint! Experience will of course increase in time and assist this process.

Contingency allowances are a regular feature of all production budgets. The key is not to fall into the frequent trap of simply applying a fixed percentage. The worst case scenario is the low budget, small scale production like a profit-share on the Fringe. With a budget of £100, a 10% or 15% contingency is of little real use. What kind of emergency can be sorted out by £10? So, the contingency needs to be big enough to deal with a real situation. It must also follow that the bigger the production gets, the smaller, relatively, the contingency percentage can become because the sum of money will be substantial enough to cope with a late change and also, because large fixed price contracts are likely to have been let before the budget went 'live'.

Monitoring expenditure throughout the production process is essential. Ideally, it is ongoing, but it ought to happen at least at a series of fixed points. It is also important to decide the point where a cost item enters the calculation. A system of logging expenditure as it is incurred is very helpful. 'Incurred' means that at the point an order or instruction is made, the money is, effectively, spent. The arrival of the invoice at some further date, and the subsequent issuing of payment of it, are far too random events to be reliable for budgetary reporting. Remember, budgeting and control are not the same as accounting. Anyone empowered to issue an order should establish the cost of the order and at the point of the order put that sum into the calculation. When the account from the supplier does arrive, if it varies from the incurred sum, it should be questioned.

The usual columns of budget show estimates and, often, accrued totals at certain points. What is also useful is a 'projected actual' figure. This is established from available data when expenditure under any one budget heading is nearly complete, or has a lot of fixed costs e.g. contracts. If the 'projected actual figure is higher than the original budget, then some of the contingency is already being spent. Equally, if it is under budget, then the available contingency may be getting larger.

In the days of manual scribing we could draw a line through a sum and write a revision above or below. With spreadsheets the new figure can instantly supplant the old. But a danger may lurk therein. The printout will not show the older figure which is useful for logging trends expecially in rapid escalation and may help form judgements. Make sure a print is taken of each stage.

This knowledge, whichever way it is expressed, is enormously useful in assessing when and how far to dip into contingency funds or move funds across headings.

There is also a matter of cash flow. Not all managements treat this in the same way and one can find oneself in the dark like a cultivated mushroom waiting for some fertiliser to be dropped around. However, on a big production where lots of work is being put to contract having access to money is extremely useful. I'm a firm believer in paying a percentage up front for works to be done. It should enable the contractor to aquire the materials to get on with the work. So it is very useful to know how the money is set up. It can be a mixture of cash, bank facility, or staged payments, or there may be 'in kind' aspects like free rehearsal space. Obviously, when purchasing off-the-peg items, the supplier does not expect payment before delivery; more likely 30 days after invoice. So there is an available control factor here; you can restrain the urge to have everything ready to hand and take delivery just before it is really needed. In this way the time the management is exposed to the full cost of the production can be kept down if payments can be made after the opening.

This leads to defining who has authority to incur expenditure. Presumably set, lighting, props, etc. are large headings with sub-headings to each. Rule 1 should be that any one department cannot incur expenditure on behalf of another. Whoever receives and logs expenditure should then be made aware of the perimeter of each department's spending profile.

Secondly, try not to have any kind of general 'catch all' column, e.g. it doesn't matter if 'access equipment hire' appears in three or four different departments because each department total will reflect their own needs or demands. If there were a general 'catch all' column, the temptation would be there to keep the equipment 'in any case' because it wouldn't be adding to their budget.

Experience has got to play a role in delivering the 'gut' response managements always seem to want when one first has a look at a new model. Remembering past experience, balancing the perceived complexity or variance from normal, will come into making the answer. Production Managers need to keep cost parameters ever present in their heads.

Next there is a rough Budget Totals sheet. By the time you get this far many other pieces of paper or pages on a screen will have been processed. The important thing is that however it looks it should fit snugly the show being worked upon. It should feel comfy. Forsee all likely events and even the less likely and make sure that whatever the costs there is a home for them on the page. There are notes to this as well which will probably be read before these words. Lastly are lists of the kind of budget headings which have been found useful at some time or other. These are by no means exhaustive.

- The Totals Sheet should reflect established circumstances. Each heading should be for a discrete sector of work.
- Separate sheets are needed for the different sectors.
- Agreed Estimate. Having decided on contractors or suppliers, further talks should produce a detailed price, to be reflected in the documentation.
- Incurred – as budget items are ordered or contracted, the relevant sum of money becomes 'incurred'. This column also shows what the liability would be if the project was cancelled – for any reason. It needs regular updating.
- The projected actual (PA) will initially be the total of agreed estimates. As real information re: incurred expenditure becomes available, the PA figure for the heading may move up or down. If it moves up, then the contingency figure must be reduced accordingly. If the contingency evaporates – sound the alarm. Don't plan to spend the contingency.
- If PA is consistently adrift from estimate, there is a problem at the beginning – sound the alarm.
- Avoid going 'live' until all needs are catered for in the budget.
- Personnel – Fees - consultants, safety, listed building advice, etc.
- Direct – Hourly paid assistance, draughting, production tech crew (not paid by theatre) etc. Designers and creative fees are not usually in the PM budget

    NB: Care is needed when allocating contingency. Expenditure should not go into both the Incurred column and the department columns, as a variation of the agreed estimate. The totals at the bottom of the right hand columns are the working tools.
- Each item on the list required should fit one of the headings.
- Include hires for fixed runs.
- Props and Costume usually represent the largest number of separate purchases. This can become a very long set of separate pages.
- Transport. Each sector will incur some costs. They should be kept in their own sectors except for movements of the whole production.

	Original Estimates	Agreed Estimates	Incurred	Projected Actual
SCENERY				
COSTUME				
PROPERTIES				
LIGHTING				
TRANSPORT (WHOLE SHOW)				
SOUND				
RENT/HIRES Rehearsal Rooms Access Equipment Storage etc.				
PERSONNEL Fees				
Direct				
BUILDING WORKS				
CONTINGENCY				
TOTALS		DATE		

A simplified Budget Totals form

SET	PROPS	LIGHT	SOUND
Timber inc. boards	Carpets/rugs	New Equipment	Studio Time
Steel stock	Bought furniture	Colour	Artistes Time
Softs - cloths etc. (contract)	Materials	Gobos	Short term Hires
Softs - canvas etc. (by metre)	Tools	Cleaning Materials	Recording materials
Ironmongery	Cleaning materials	Sundries	Rights/Royalties
Engineering components	Polishing materials	Art Work	Instrument Hire
Scenic contracts	Collections	Slides/ Mov Images	Travel
Engineering contracts	Dressings	FX	Comms
Access Equipment	Access Equipment	Access Equipment	Access Equipment
Paints and glues	Food	Engineering	Voltage Variation
Workshop rent	Consumables	Bells, Buzzers	Software
Packaging	Packaging	Packaging	Research
Collections	Junk	Collections	Collections
Storage	Practicals	Testing Equipment	Testing Equipment
Tools	Contracts	Contracts	Contracts
Textures	Workshop rent	Cue Systems	
Flocking	Storage	Software	
Lifting Gear	Research		
Welding	Soft furnishings		
	Bells		
	Door Furniture		
	Crashes		

Checklist of Budget Headings – by no means exhaustive!

It Gets Better With Experience
(a cricketing analogy)

Many years ago while fielding at mid off, I collected a wild throw-in from fine leg and the batsman set off from the bowler's end for a second run. I threw low and flat over the stumps and the wicket keeper did the necessary – an unexpected wicket given that the original fielder had actually not done too well. For the next few years or so, aware of this extra opportunity, I waited, alert, at mid off. When it did happen again, I saw it earlier and completed the job more efficiently, re-running the sequence in my mind.

There is nothing that we do that should be put in the brain dustbin. Often if you re-run a sequence a few years later with more knowledge or experience, fresh answers appear that weren't apparent the first time.

Some People Don't Want to be Helped

A designer friend had been asked to design a new musical being premiered at one of London's larger off-West End venues. From what he told me there was a degree of naivety evident among the authors and the rest of the concept team. Someone must have said something because not long afterwards I was asked to see the 'manager', who seemed to be the literary agent as well. He said they realised that they would need a Production Manager and would I do it. Of course – one rarely turns down work.

So we had a theatre, a design, a lighting design, a reasonable but not generous budget, and enthusiasm. As rehearsals evolved the overlying design concept became stressed. Changes were made and the budget was stretched without too much grief. Personalities started to clash and the director and MD were replaced. Phrases like 'save the show' were heard daily.

The new MD maintained that the sound mix arranged by his predecessor was at fault – only a massive new sound system would do. "Get it," they said. I did. The normal constraint of a Production Manager – budget – disappeared. I became a money conduit. We opened, many times over the original figure. Nobody seemed to mind.

We were not a hit. The inhibitors of cloud cuckoo land spoke of a transfer to a more amenable venue. I had to say I had other pressing engagements.

My designer friend who'd shared this experience then found out, bit by bit, that the senior personnel all seemed to be linked to a large film-making company. The show must have been for them a fun way of burning of the profits, but for me it was the only time that a management took no notice whatsoever of the usual cautionary rationale of the Production Manager. Without the usual rules, I wondered why they needed me at all!

Going Dutch

Just a few years ago I was called at the last minute to take over the lighting of a production in Holland. The producing company was resident in a large city and had as a home base a modern, well-equipped civic theatre. The crew structure was different from what you might expect in a UK regional producing theatre and the role of stage management was certainly cut up into differently shaped slices.

The production in question, *Tartuffe,* was destined to have, for reasons which still remain obscure, a remote controlled table. The company's technical staff had completed this feat in-house, by the ingenious use of a radio remote control system for model aeroplanes linked to components of an electrical wheelchair. A lot of amusement was had as the drive unit was scudded about the stage area by an operator wiggling a joystick in the prompt corner.

The technical team took me to their workshop area, where it became clear that they had a policy of keeping all engineering components which had been built into the machinery for different productions. There were shelves of bearings, pulleys, castors, wheels, sprockets, chains, gearboxes, etc. They smilingly explained that, where possible, they would re-use any one of these components and frequently were able to re-jig the designs so that they could reduce the cost of new materials.

One of the company's forthcoming productions was to be Shaw's *Captain Brassbound's Conversion.* The setting, in the captain's cabin of a large sailing vessel, had an array of windows which were leaning outward over the sea, so to speak, one or two of which had to break during the action. The Dutch technicians had set up an experimental jig with a window frame set at just the angle of the set, where they were experimenting with the fixing and the impact characteristics of the breaking window pane, by using different translucent materials or means of effecting the "break". One could not fail to be impressed by the diligence and thoroughness by which this highly skilled team went about their work. At first glance, one might think that they were a bit plodding. But their methodical, linear approach to solutions meant that only very rarely did anything not work precisely as expected or as planned. It would give any Production Manager a great feeling of security to know that his team, at every level, were leaving nothing to chance.

If there is a moral, it would be that paying for additional skills up front may save a lot of expensive time at a crucial point in productions.

7 CRITICAL PATH ANALYSIS

These are the buzz words for watching the dominoes fall over. Whatever you call it, it is an essential part of most forms of management and especially so in the tight constraints of the theatre. To be effective it is a continuous activity, the mind-set being adjusted every time a new piece of information comes to light. Automatically this should translate into questioning whether or not any instructions need to be altered, and if it is necessary, the degree of urgency. It is not simplistic and has many facets. Let us now look at some of the factors separately.

The Nature of the Job

I always see things as separate tasks which combine to make a completed project or object. One should ask if the separate tasks are interdependent or not and, if they are, is the interdependence to do with time or more to do with the interface of different trades. Scale, in the sense of size, also plays a big part in defining how tasks are carried out. For instance, I can mow the lawn myself by pushing the mower up and down if the lawn is not too big. How do you define 'too big'? For the individual time will be a key factor, i.e. is the time taken to mow the lawn and the frequency it will be required going to fit into the general pattern of life of the mowing person? This will depend on what other things the mower has to do or wants to do. Cutting the grass on a fine day in fresh air can also induce a sense of well being which may encourage one to do it anyway even if it impinges on the time that should be used for other things. This leads to a syndrome known as displacement therapy whereby we avoid tasks *we don't like* by doing things *we do like* leaving no time for the unattractive job!

If the job is 'too big' but still has to be done then some decision has to be taken. This usually means going down one of two paths. The first is capital expenditure which could be the purchase of a mower with a wider cut thereby reducing the number of walks up and down the lawn. However, the person would have to work a bit harder leaving him more weary and less able to do the other things on the agenda. A motorised mower would be one further step up speeding the process and allowing the 'mower' to enjoy the experience and the fun of driving the machine as well. Of course the exercise aspect gets lost but there is always a price to progress.

The second path would be to pay someone else to do it. This too can work in two ways. I can simply employ someone to use my existing machine, justifying the expense by assuming that the person will expect less money than I would earn for the time consumed, so rendering it somehow affordable. Or, I can engage a contractor who will use his own equipment. In both of these cases the lawn cutting has to be paid for on a regular basis and needs to be built into the budget like the groceries. There is some advantage in using a contractor because he should absorb the costs of the equipment and you won't have any repair costs either. Further, because the contractor only makes money when the job is done he will want to do as many lawns as possible. It is in his interest to be quick and efficient which will minimise the disruption to the household. The direct labourer on the other hand may see that his agreed rate pays best if more time is spent pushing the mower.

Consider then that the second option does two things: it releases time which can be diverted to other profitable purposes or otherwise; but it also presupposes that the cash flow will bear the regular outgoing. The capital option is more suitable for windfall situations where lumps of money suddenly become available on a one-off basis.

All of this analogy is 'small scale'. As things grow in scale many of the basic principles still apply. Because the likes of the lawn-mowing contractor need to maximise the amount of time they spend carrying out contracts he will look for durable equipment with low maintenance requirements and means of speedily transporting it about with easy systems for loading and unloading. Skilled self-employed bricklayers who employ their own labourer to mix the cement, carry the bricks and rearrange the trestles etc. fall into the same category. Thus the skilled man can do what he does best – lay lots of bricks quickly and accurately. If a large building project is undertaken then the bricklayer microcosm needs to be repeated many times over if the project is the be finished within a reasonable time scale. Here, of course, we enter the realms of diminishing marginal returns. If there are too many bricklayers they will get in each others way and their labourers will get confusing instructions about where the scaffolds need to be. So as organisations grow the need for efficient management increases and the amount of time and effort spent on management grows exponentially. The function of management is to plan for the maximum number of skilled workers to be working without getting in each others way.

The worst case scenario is where space is so cramped that the worker has to be alone, such as a bricklayer, again, making one of those little compartments under the pavement for the electricity company or the cable TV people to keep clusters of connections or terminals. The poor chap is crouching, often unable to turn around, and using heavy engineering bricks as well. On a brick by brick basis this must be as slow as it gets but no better method has yet been found. He is effectively beyond managing.

In the light of all the above consider a stage to be a workshop. Everybody has work to do here. The problem is that they can't all do it at once, but at the same time the eventual product has to involve all disciplines – not least the performers. Luckily there is a kind of received wisdom about how fit-ups should proceed. The danger is in not submitting each new production to some kind of analysis. All productions are different in some way. Will the usual pattern suffice or is the work load on this occasion rather more for one department than usual? If it is, how is the variation likely to manifest itself?

Stages too are different and some of them work a lot better than others. The same factors apply as for the man laying bricks in a hole. There are cases in the so called fringe theatre where one individual does virtually everything in a small space. To increase the number of crew would not help because they would be getting in each other's way. There has to be some kind of correlation between the number of people required for efficient working and the working area. In a really large venue it can also be that excessive time is spent just getting from one place to another which is counter productive and expensive.

Be clear about the task in hand. This applies equally to the lone worker or the massive crew. See the whole process as a series of objectives. Even if someone is working on their own they should always be clear as to what the current objective is. This may hint at one of the cardinal differences between professional and non-professional theatre. Non-professionals often enjoy being part of the process and so linger about even if they are not strictly needed, so the objectivity of the process becomes obscured. Professionals are much happier coming to work to complete a task and then leaving to allow others to get on with their part of the work.

Critical path analysis in my view leads to separating the tasks and objectives up into controllable chunks and ordering the work so that at no time is anybody prevented from progress by competing activity or preparatory work not having been done. It means looking at the nature of each task in the way we looked at the lawn cutting exercise. If there is a problem of some sort – how can it be resolved? Is it something which can be remedied by more labour *or* is it going to be helped by capital injection? Going back to our bricklayer in the hole, or anything like it, the best thing for him is to allow him enough time so that he can absorb a few hiccups in the process i.e. to recognise that he cannot be significantly helped. The capital input might be a new tool or piece of access equipment which would allow the work to be completed more quickly. Sometimes a rule is best broken. A scenery contractor may issues drawings to the men on the benches but if a complex three dimensional piece has to be made it may be more efficient to give the model to a skilled craftsman who will design the structure as he goes along, saving complex draughting.

There is much variety and sophistication in industry. Some companies exist solely to carry out very specific tasks. Given that people work most efficiently at what they know best, the work needs to be appraised in that light. We often get challenged to deal with new materials or new applications of old ones. There could be sense in separating out some specific aspect and giving it to a contractor who will do it with the benefit of experience which we don't have. Balance this against the extra time taken by inexperienced staff with its cost implications of wasted raw material – or, equally costly, the purchase or lease of specialised equipment which will not normally be required.

These issues bear on different departments in different ways and it is worth looking at how they look in the different disciplines.

Lighting

Lighting is a factor in almost every production one can think of but, from an equipment point of view, each installation is likely to carry more similarities than scenery or costume. It can be useful to look at lighting equipment as a kind of adult meccano. This may not be popular with the practitioners but from a management point of view it holds true. The process breaks down into three main elements: rigging, focusing and plotting. They do need to be done in order but it is possible to place other work in between them. The conditions required are different. Rigging can take place in work light while other work is progressing, provided of course that there is enough space. The process finishes when lighting and scenic staff come together to establishing final position by setting deads. Focusing is best done in dark conditions and requires that elements of the setting germane to the focusing be present in their correct locations. Stage management presence is often useful for the precise placing of furniture or where performers put themselves for certain scenes. Finally, plotting cues requires the full scenic picture in its best sense. Other members of the artistic team may want to be present whether or not the plotting is being done on its own or 'over' a rehearsal.

This is what it looks like from the outside. But to manage the process greater depth is needed. Rigging breaks down into a number of instruments which, 99% of the time, will be suspended from horizontal pipes or bars, suspended from brackets attached to vertical tubes or mounted vertically on some kind of stand. The equipment to do all this is well known and readily available. A competent production electrician can work out from a rig plan precisely what equipment is needed and have it ready before the work commences.

Experienced staff can rig quite quickly because they are doing a fairly repetitive task working towards a foreseeable objective. The rig plan will tell exactly how many instruments are required and if the crew have worked together before in the same venue they should have an idea of the time likely to be needed. The factors noted further above apply – namely, non-productive time spent going from A to B in a big venue or cramped conditions created by an intensive rig and a set being put up at the same time impeding and slowing the work in a smaller one. The critical path must have an acceptable time slot for the rig to be completed. If this is problematical the usual recourse is for additional crew or re-scheduling so as to avoid clashes with other work or workers. The capital spend option is rarely valid because of the individual handling required by each instrument.

When we get to focusing firmer ground should appear. There should be less interruption to the flow, as the preparatory work has been done. Almost invariably access equipment will need to be moved about. This may involve others moving scenery to clear a path and cross-departmental liaison. However it does tend to boil down to one individual, the lighting designer. This person must have a very clear concept of what is required of each instrument. The lighting designer has the unenviable job of having to be creative in full view of all present who will all be aware of the time being taken. Nevertheless from our management point of view we need to set aside a reasonable time for the focus. One way is to allow say 90 seconds or two minutes per instrument and multiply the time by the number of lanterns in the rig. This may sound a bit stentorian but as rigs tend to get bigger the economics haven't grown to allow an exponential increase in time. Some luminaires just require pointing and maybe a barn door tweaked into place. They should take less than a minute if both the lighting designer and the focuser are alert to the task. This leaves more time for the more complex adjustments to profiles or projectors. For this all to work the crew must concentrate on ensuring that someone is always ready with another instrument just as soon as one is finished. This activity can be accelerated by more personnel, but the skill profile has to be correct. The less experienced people will probably end up moving access equipment or ferrying piles of colour filters.

This leaves the plotting. From early on, within reason the number of states and cues should be known. Many designers can give a rough estimate of the number of new states they can create in an hour, based of course on the size of the rig and the variety potential i.e. colour changers or moving lights that need to be programmed as well as level settings. We can assume that blackout cues and returns to state should take no real time at all. So the time frame has to be worked out on the basis of the needs of the show. The other factor is the set or settings. If they have to change then crew will have to be present. Again, analyse. If it is a three act piece with three separate sets then wisdom dictates doing it in reverse so that act one is left onstage ready for the next rehearsal. The crew can be released once it has been set, leaving the lighting team and stage management to finish the plotting. This, like focusing, relies heavily on the designer whose creative juices will effectively control the pace of the work. It is important to provide the peripheral services, like set or prop moves, quickly so that the flow of the work is maintained. Lastly, remember that designers are human and need rest and sustenance! Experience tells that it is far better to plan plotting to begin at the start of a day or at the very least when the designer and the electrics crew are well rested. It is not an activity best done when tired.

The Company

Yes, the performing company have to form part of the Production Manager's critical path. Part of our work has got to be to allow for the maximum time to be spent fine tuning a production once it has been set up in a theatre. This entails ensuring that everything – yes everything – that can be done beforehand *is* done beforehand. All too often one hears the casual phrase: "Oh, we'll sort that out at the technical rehearsal". It needs to be stamped out as a philosophy and modus operandum. Where the company is concerned it means developing a close relationship with stage management and the director or the designer. The designer can be a useful ally because problems caused by the company can adversely effect the amount of time to be spent dressing the set – which will help focus his attention onto the problem areas.

Be clear; what we are trying to avoid are hold ups during any kind of onstage rehearsal owing to lack of preparedness in the company. This results in time not being best used but often, and far worse, it costs money. The entire complement of show crew are present and the clock is ticking.

What are the problem areas? Manual dexterity is probably the least obvious but one of the most frequent reasons for hold ups in rehearsal caused by the company. Despite many years of experience, in some cases actors do tense up when working, rendering simple everyday tasks a little more difficult. There is the prop man's phrase 'actor proof' which takes this phenomenon into account. It is counteracted by making things more durable or unbreakable, and able to withstand harsher treatment than one might expect. Into this category fall door latches and locks, practical curtains, luggage and such things as soda siphons. The main objective must always be to minimise and simplify the handling of practical equipment by performers.

There are two worst-case scenarios. Firstly there are situations where an actor is confronting something they have never done before – which could be almost anything. I remember a full technical rehearsal being held up when it was discovered that a young actor had never opened a bottle of champagne – which his character was required to do. Perhaps everyone assumed that everyone knows how to do this, but it was an expensive assumption. This same scenario also covers more complex machinery and equipment such as weapons, scientific apparatus or even sporting gear.

The second 'worst-case' has got to be food and drink. It is never easy and the tense-up factor can really get into its stride. The situation is not helped by the fact that there are some well known food scenes, like the cucumber sandwich sequence in *The Importance of Being Earnest*. It can't be avoided; it has to be tackled. The answer in both of these cases is rehearsal, well in advance and done to the point where the margins of error are not a factor.

Mechanical scenery and stage machinery also require careful integration. There is of course the safety aspect but there is also the appearance factor. The director needs to be able to envisage the moving sequences. This requires close liaison between the whole team so that the Production Manager is reassured that what is being rehearsed is within the scope of the equipment to be used or being made. This can mean providing additional rehearsal equipment well beforehand, in the form of canvas pieces representing the moving parts. Stage management will make sure that the director is in the right relationship to the action. There have been some hilarious reviews describing artistes chasing pieces of furniture or scenery across the stage where clearly the objective rehearsal had not taken place. It may sound simplistic but it's worth checking little things like which way a door swings because actors may be miming the most convenient thing for them which may or may not be correct.

From the Production Management point of view what we want of the company arriving onstage for the first time is to feel no sense of culture shock or unease. This will allow the time to be usefully spent integrating with the likes of light and sound which do not come within the bounds of rehearsal rooms. The process of critical path analysis here is to identify the problem areas and make sure that they are covered before the move to the stage so that a large slab of time does not have to be set aside for acclimatisation. Of course there will always be exceptions like Mother Courage's cart, but if you are doing that play it will be a known factor and should not be a surprise.

Wardrobe

As someone who spent much of his active career working on the stage or in stage related activities, Wardrobe has always held a degree of mystique. It is a fascinating discipline and I have more than once had cause to smile when the Wardrobe Mistress suggests that it is usually the wardrobe department who design the rear side of any costume.

Because a lot of costume seems to be derived from modes of period dress, there is always the potential of continued use for costumes, either as hire or sale. For this reason, it seems that in many cases there is no point in creating poorer quality costumes because, by their nature, they are relatively easy to store and are much more likely to have an after-life than scenery, for example. To a degree the same arguments apply to props. Again, because of the nature of the work, it is more frequent to find costumiers working at home or in small units, rather than having to have large workshop premises.

With the plethora of hire companies and other specialist suppliers to the clothing trade, there are always a number of options available when it comes to costuming a production. Some companies who maintain a wardrobe stock will seek to use much of what they already have and augment as necessary. Decisions will need to be made as to whether all the costumes are to be made, or whether some will be hired or, in some cases, even purchased if they are close to modern tailoring trends.

As ever, time is of course going to be of the essence. Each costume will normally need to be assembled from its various component parts, so that a 'fitting' can take place, and the costume designer will normally want to be present at the fitting. The question then becomes: "How available is the designer for this, and how many individual costumes will have to be seen by the designer before they are moved towards finishing?" This may also have a bearing on the length of the rehearsal period and whether the company are rehearsing within close proximity of where the costumes are being made, or are at some distance. Wardrobe personnel, perhaps more so than the other technical departments, seem to have developed an expertise for bringing things together from various different sources

From a Production Management point of view, the key questions will be:
- Whether or not the costumes need to be seen on stage under lighting conditions by the designer before a technical rehearsal, or whether the costumes present a safety hazard or issue, ie: are people wearing garments which they are so unfamiliar with that they may endanger themselves?
- Are there actions on stage, especially where flights of steps or ramps are concerned, where cast in costume should go through their routines before a full rehearsal, thereby obviating the problem of doing this while the full crew is present?
- Are there aspects of the costuming which require the presence of costume or practice costume at rehearsal and are the wardrobe kitted out to do this, or does a special plan need to be set up?

Close liaison is required here between production and stage management to assess the practicalities involved.

Some of the processes in costume involve the purchase of fabric, the subsequent dyeing the fabric, or in some way distressing the fabric, mean that there will be a significant period of time following the purchase before the actual making of the costume can be started. This is important because it may well be that the fabrication of the costumes should begin well before rehearsals commence. But of course it is always going to be difficult if the wardrobe personnel do not know who the performers are and, therefore, will not have measurements for the costumes. However, as noted above, in these cases it may require engagement of a larger number of individuals to make costumes over a shorter period rather than a smaller number making the costumes over a longer period.

Costumes then are an assemblage of items which the actor wears. Wardrobe requires a lot of detailed listing to ensure that all of a character's articles are in the same dressing room with him. This is standard practice but it is as well to check from time to time that that the costumiers are on schedule in every way.

Stage Department

For our purposes here, it is probably best to separate Stage into two sections. In the first section we should deal with the Stage Department working in the theatre, and the second section should deal with the process of manufacturing scenery, etc.

Stage staff in theatres deal with a number of fairly routine activities. These will include moving scenery, folding drapes, hanging drapes, loading transports, etc. By their routine nature, skilled staff can perform these actions with a high degree of efficiency. The theatre, in Britain at least, relied for many years on a diet of touring whereby productions went into a theatre in the morning and opened to the public on the very same evening. This was made possible by efficient crews in the provincial touring theatres.

A crew installing drapes for a concert or variety performance will take very little time to do so if it is part of their regular style of activity. If the drapes are in house, they will know them fairly well and the work should proceed smoothly. Equally, for many years repertory theatres relied largely on stocks of scenery (flats) which were assembled in different patterns for each new production, having been repainted from their previous design, whatever that might have been. Although the crews in repertory theatres would tend to be smaller because their work span was slightly longer, the activity was routine and straightforward.

Stage is the one area of our work where, especially if one considers the Flying Department to be part of it, manpower plays the key role. Large items of scenery or drapes cannot be easily or efficiently handled by two or three people. So, to an extent, the size of the articles will indicate how many people need to be involved. Modern safety considerations have added greater importance to this.

In days gone by there were rather more theatres where 'get ins' were described as difficult. This usually meant longer carries, or lifts, or awkward facets of the building which had to be negotiated. The ideal must be a large space whereby the incoming equipment can be quickly taken to designated areas around the space without having to go round or through or under other things. The advice of those close to the situation is invaluable.

Unlike a luminaire, or item of sound equipment, for instance, scenery is specific in its location, i.e. every single piece of scenery is destined for a specific place on the stage. Thus, it is important that the personnel are well provided with advance information so that, as things arrive, they can be distributed in such a way as to ease the next process of work, i.e. it is not sensible to have things stuck directly against the wall if they are going to be the first things you want when you have finished unloading.

So, the first part of the analysis at this stage must be how much scenery and other equipment is going to have to arrive at the same time and, having got it all in, is there likely to be a reasonable space left over for installation work to begin?

On productions which take a long time to install, frequently parts of the set or installation arrive at different times, so that there isn't a distinct 'get in' period. This process can mean that the work of one contractor getting in can interrupt the work of another contractor undertaking an installation. Or, if the rehearsal process has already started, the arrival of new pieces of the installation has to be 'jigged around' the rehearsal process to avoid interruption. In some worst cases, the get-in doors are poorly placed, so that they almost invariably cause a disruption or force things to be moved on to the acting area to provide a pathway.

This may seem a rather laborious approach to the subject, but it needs to be remembered that if the work area is completely cluttered with scenery and equipment for a production, the installation process will be slowed down by having to move the cluttered equipment about on a regular basis in order to create workspace. One recognises that this is only likely to occur on particularly large installations, either for commercial or large scale touring operations. However, it is a factor that does need to be borne in mind if it is at all possible, so that some of the equipment can be kept on its transport, or in dock, until some of the early arrivals have been installed in their places.

Because scenery is so specific and knowledge of it so essential, consideration also needs to be given to personnel. It is no accident that large crews tend to divide themselves down the centre of the stage and operate under specific 'charge hands' either side of the stage. Large numbers of men cannot be organised effectively by one individual and a tiered structure appears to work well. Thus, large touring presentations have always taken numbers of skilled personnel well versed in the production with them, so that they can give clear and accurate instructions to the labour force provided in local theatres.

It was noted above that there are a number of routine functions, however stage work is more likely than most others to have to deal with extraordinary functions. This is because designers always like to experiment with new materials and methods in order to create different visual images on the stage. One remembers early stories of crews encountering items of scenery made with fibre glass, or the hazards of working with fire retardant Perspex. This, then, requires a longer period of consideration as means and ways are worked out for handling the complex, the large, the awkward or the unusual. This is where time needs to be allowed for a more cautious approach. Within the routine tasks, it may well be possible for people to work slightly faster, but this is not possible when they are doing something which is new to them.

The stage department is also unusual insofar that on large productions more members of that department than any other may well be involved in moving items during the course of the performance, even in sight of the audience. In some cases this means that there has to be an element of training, attendance at rehearsals, and so on. This will naturally affect the production process because instead of being released as rehearsals commence, they have to remain on standby which may affect the amount of hours they can usefully put into finishing off any uncompleted parts of the scenery installation. Of course, it is simpler if the scene changes take place behind the lowered tabs, where the activity does not have to be choreographed. Nevertheless, it does require that the crew remain present in the building should they be called upon to change the scenery at any time.

Here, too, one has to again step back and analyse the situation. If it is a production with scenery moving in sight of the audience, it is likely that on the first occasion a considerable amount of time will be spent orchestrating these movements and writing out the relevant plots for those crew members involved. Subsequent installations or repeats of the process should take less time because the plots exist, although they may require small variations.

The same thing can apply to finally setting the appearance of the stage when borders and other things are being 'deaded'. Here, obviously, there is a design input and just as with a lighting designer doing his focusing, the designer will effectively be driving the process. A designer who is clear and concise in his thinking will be faster and more efficient than someone who is less clear either in what they want, or how to go about getting what they want. This is where a proactive Production Management can play a role. The Production Manager may well have to work towards clarifying what the designer wants and converting that into information which can push the process forward more quickly.

When we started talking about the stage department in respect of critical path analysis, we noted that it fell roughly into two sections. So far, we have discussed the stage department at work within a theatre or venue. The second section will be the building of scenery and specialised equipment. It has been alluded to elsewhere that it remains pertinent to note that in the main lighting and sound equipment tends to be manufactured for purchase on an off-the-peg basis, whilst stage, wardrobe and props are much more specific in their relationship to the overall design of any one production.

To get a grip on this process it is sensible (as it so often is) to work backwards. The finished product usually arrives on stage fresh from the attentions of the scenic artists. It is essential to get some feedback from the painters. Productions with complex *trompe-l'oeil*, figurative painting may well take rather longer with the scenic artists than those where large areas of monochrome are being prepared. Further, where the figurative painting is concerned, the artists often prefer to work as individuals on single large pieces or canvases, although they may use assistants to lay in the base colour washes. Scenic artists, like lighting designers, can usually offer some indication as to the length of time required to complete the task being contemplated. It will of course be affected by the size of the work and its relation to the space in which it is to be carried out, i.e. if there is a paint frame and the artist has plenty of access to it, then he can be fairly accurate; if it is something which has to be built up in the scenic painting area, then obviously this will take time to build and the artist will spend some considerable time organising access equipment round it in order to reach it for painting.

Other factors which can affect painting will be applications of textures or other compounds and substances, before the final paint surface is applied. In some cases these react very quickly and in others they require significant time to dry. So one has to take a fairly clear view on this and mentally separate the forthcoming production into those pieces which are reasonably conventional, i.e. flat and accessible, from those which are unconventional, such as those requiring treatment other than fairly standard painting processes, or present problems of access or other nature.

Remember here also that not everyone is the same; there are some artists who are good at certain types of work and some better at other types of work and, if time is going be a pressure, it will always be best to offer the artist a project he knows and enjoys doing rather than something he will perhaps make a rather good job of in the end, but take longer in the process. Nevertheless, it is this appraisal of how long things will take going through the paint process that informs the critical path of the building. Obviously, as mentioned above, if part of the show is fairly flat, then that is best done early so it can be packed to the side and not occupy space which may be required for complex three-dimensional items to be painted last of all.

It is important here, too, to be very clear as to what state the scenery will be in when it arrives at the painter's.

The key is to what degree the scenery will have been 'fitted'. Will all the pieces have been assembled and then disassembled, so that they are easy to reassemble on the paint frame? Equally, it is not unknown for scenic artists to apply textures etc. on surfaces which are due to abut on to others, thereby creating problems later down the line. The most simplistic situation is where the painter simply paints a tie-on backcloth which can be delivered directly to the painters from the manufacturer without going near the scenic fabricator at all.

Still working backwards, we need to consider that several scenic workshops may be engaged, or only one. If it is one, then the conversation can be held with a single individual to create the best flow of work to achieve the desired effect. If there are several, it may well be that the individual scenic shops may not be able to do the work in the order most convenient for them, because the order of materials required by the painters may not allow for that. The question can become: "Is there a price for inconvenience and is it worth paying?"

The process of letting contracts is dealt with elsewhere, but it is important at this stage to ensure that the flexibility of the individual contractor to fit into the overall plan is part of the decision-taking process.

The most awkward set of circumstances arises when the number of contractors competent and able to carry out a certain type of work is very small, in which case the Production Manager may find himself chasing space in their work schedule so as to jig other things around it. It must be clear by now that nothing should be set into action until all of these questions have been considered and addressed. This is not to say that the final answer should be carved in stone, but certainly the Production Manager must have a view as to how he wants to proceed. If there is a single specialist contractor required by the design team, and that specialist firm is particularly busy, then it may be sensible to see what bits of that work could be done, *in extremis*, by others, thus leaving the specialist to concentrate fully on the specific specialisms involved. Again, this, bears on the way the contracts are let and the interfaces between them.

It cannot be over-emphasised that it is vitally important that every individual and contractor in this process knows what is expected of them. This is especially so in these days of far greater concentration on matters of Health & Safety. Thus, it may not simply be the article which is required, but some instruction from the contractor or fabricator as to how it should be best handled once it has been passed over to others. Contractors, too, should bear in mind that their contracts will properly require them to provide information about what it is they have created in order to fulfil the risk assessment procedures that are likely to be required by other contractors in the chain and, eventually, by the crew in the theatre itself.

Overviewing the Whole Path

The easiest path to define is that of the fabricated object which needs the attention of different contractors. The path goes from the metal worker to the people who apply a timber cladding and on to the painter, etc. If each one is honest about the time needed then the painters should finish just at the moment it is required on stage. This entails no storage and reduces the likelihood of collateral damage before installation. The pinnacle of this kind of efficiency could be the construction of the Empire State Building in New York. The builders were restricted to the city block where the building was to stand and the building filled the block. So there was no place to store materials. They managed by integrating materials into the building within a few hours of delivery. Trucks arrived sequentially every 30 seconds and were allowed 150 seconds to unload the steel beams of the frame. As the structure grew the lower floors could be used for storage. All this was done well before the age of the computer and its related programmes. Human imagination was the driving force. And so it has to be with us. The unique characteristics of each production will defy the development of 'how to' floppy discs for Production Managers.

The idea is not always well received, but there is a similarity here with production line manufacturing. Cars are made on moving lines passing through areas where specific components are added to the growing vehicle. The manufacturer works out, with the benefit of experience, the order in which this happens. The personnel need to have the right tools and the length of the working area has to be long enough for the job to be done and for the worker to get back to the beginning to repeat the task. Lack of tools, components or not enough time to do the work can cause the whole system to foul up.

Think again of our production. Are we not doing something very similar? The Production Management function must include the decision when to introduce the various elements to the product. The lack of or unpreparedness of any element, and that includes the Company, can delay the whole process and adversely affect the work of others. If the car production line analogy doesn't work for you, then think of a cookery programme where the presenter has pre-prepared bowls of different ingredients which get sequentially tipped into the mix as it is stirred, heated and eventually decorated onto a plate. The sequence is decided by the cook; the Production Manager is a sort of cook, creating something for others to appreciate. This sequence is the critical path and to effectively manage we need to define it and control it. We need to develop scenarios which allow for things to go off track a bit, but we, by constant monitoring of progress on all fronts should never find ourselves being surprised.

Being surprised is not managing, it's responding to stimuli – not good.

The Fireman Wins The Game . . .

The design for *Way of the World* at the Old Vic included some flown 'representative' trees. The 'foliage' was formed of a rough hessian cut into shapes, stiffened and painted.

Well, the hessian proved pretty flammable, and various treatments were proposed. The Fire Officer agreed to visit the paint frame on a Saturday morning where Leslie Woolnough, Head of Paint Frame, would try the different mixes of fire retardant and paint, and hopefully it would be agreed one would be satisfactory.

I had some parenting duties that weekend and, in the relaxed atmosphere of a Saturday morning, I was accompanied by my 3½-year-old daughter as I popped in to see how things were getting on.

Rows of bits of hessian and cauldrons of various brews were laid out. A piece of hessian would be treated, then dried, and then the fireman would set light to it. After a little while, my curious offspring asked the fireman, "What are you doing?" The kindly officer, in uniform of course, looked down, smiled, and said: "We are playing a game and, at the moment, I'm winning!"

8 REAL EXPERIENCES

The White Devil

Sometimes there are issues besides getting the production completed in good order and on time which push the process further than one might suppose in the first instance. This happened to me on the production of *The White Devil* at the Old Vic in 1969. There had been a period of uneasy industrial relations with the staff and there was no doubt that the repertoire system put a strain on the crew. From their perspective the work load could have looked like a treadmill with long days and many nights being the norm, so the troubles were understandable to a degree, we wanted to make an effort wherever we were able, to take the angst out of the work by keeping things as bother free as possible.

In those days the National Theatre management, Laurence Olivier at the helm, categorised plays on an 'A', 'B' or 'C' basis. 'A' meant that the production would be capable of doing a matinee changeover, i.e. being set or struck in double quick time thus allowing two different plays to be presented on the same day. Please bear in mind that the Old Vic at the time did not have any significant stage machinery, other than the flying system, to ease the work. There was no adequate storage space either, so a lot of work involved loading and unloading lorries at all times and in all weathers. 'B', meant the play required a day changeover and a 'C' was so heavy or complex that a night as well as a day would be needed to get it ready. The great man had a monosyllabic expletive starting with a 'c' to describe such productions.

The White Devil was designed by Piero Gherardi, whose Italian presented linguistic challenges, to say nothing of the others. What was wanted was effectively a wall consisting of massive blocks of 'stone', two or more metres and three courses high. The cast were to use the opportunities offered by crevices to enhance the ominous nature of the drama. So far so good, but . . . the two lower courses of blocks had to move independently in and out of the line of the wall – not so simple after all. Nevertheless, from economic and an *esprit de corps* point of view, this production could not afford to be a 'C' and an easy 'B' was what was needed. Of course, none of this was of any interest to the designer – why should it be?

The 'model' was a polyurethane casting of the wall, not to scale. We decided to get some broad ranging decisions first. The second row of 'stones' would be on a bridge, a single span nearly the width of the prosc opening. Performers were to use the platform as well. Peter Kemp, stage engineer supreme, thought it was feasible – just. Memory tells me that up to seven blocks approximately two metres high all had to move independently on the bridge.

The system of driving trucks via a lug or tongue going through a slot in the floor and linking to a winched skate on a track below was an obvious answer. It had been around for some time and was reliable, if not sophisticated. It would do for the moves required in the performance, but I was worried about the installation time. My experience recalled lots of fiddling and time consuming terminations being made with wire rope grips when setting this kind of mechanism – it could therefore cause a problem for the repertoire changeover.

In the meantime, the lower row of blocks was resolving into a series of totally independent pieces which were going to perform a kind of choreography. They could be pushed directly by the crew, who could lurk behind them or retreat upstage behind masking hanging from the upstage side of the bridge. The only real issue was keeping the blocks in place on the steep rake. Bolts and bolt holes were part of the answer. One block, for no apparent logical reason, seemed to suffer all kinds of demands as rehearsals proceeded, including that of being able to revolve and move completely downstage of the rest of the wall. Two of the crew set up house in this Block 'B', which became the topic of several witty cartoons backstage. The revolve move was simplicity itself – a 'foot' with a rotating bearing was attached to the end of a piece of threaded studding. A sub-frame located it at the centre of the block. On cue, the 'foot' could be wound down until it just took the weight of the block and became the point around which it would turn. The men inside just had to walk it round to the next position.

Given that the lower blocks were not appearing to be mechanically problematic, attention turned elsewhere. The edges of the wall were not really defined on the model so we had to work out for ourselves the simplest surround which could continue the ethic of the wall to a point where it ran out of audience sight. The designer's only instruction was that there should be 'more wall'! The header became a hard border with a soffit covered in carved polystyrene. This could just about be flown out on changeover.

However, the bridge still needed more thought. It was going to be slung between two piers, one either side of the stage. The upstage edge, never seen, carried a handrail which also provided vertical bracing to stop sag in the middle. The visible leading edge would need to be a fairly solid beam in order to be strong enough not to bend in the middle. The blocks which were to sit on it were different widths, so the weight would not be evenly distributed.

The movement was revisited. I wanted to keep the system integral to the structure if possible, i.e. I wanted to avoid the wires to and from the winches having to run into the area upstage of the wall, which would be busy with the moving blocks and their movers. The answer was to take the wires to the support piers either side. We decided that a trial erection (sic) would be a worthwhile investment. Luckily, Sadlers Wells had some spare time and we set up there for a couple of days. The results, as far as flex/sag factors in the main bridge were concerned, were very good, leaving Peter Kemp with only some reworking of the tensions in the front beam.

But the moving mechanism for the structure continued to

The Whie Devil: the actors are standing on a bridge devoid of any supports in the middle. The lower stones were free to move in, out and sideways in the space underneath. The stones behind the actors were on tracks which provided the drive for back and forth movement.

worry me; the wires had to divert first laterally to one of the side piers, and then down to an individual helical winch drum for each block. I could still see lots of cursing people pushing ends of wire through pulleys, having to fit rope grips to ends of wire which got more frayed every time the thing was set up. I then remembered ladies' figure skates where, as the boot reaches up to the calf, the laces pass around little hooks instead of through holes. Here I was looking at a situation where the wires were only under tension when a move was being made. If the wire came off the pulley, the worst thing that could happen would be that the block would not be able to move. Why couldn't we chop part of the shroud off the pulleys so that the wires just bent around them? This was done.

The track which was to hold the 'skate' was effectively a box section with a slot in it. We cut a notch out of the box and inserted the 'skate' from the top with its wires attached. At the downstage end there was a return pulley. If this could be made easily removable, then it would be a simple matter to slip the bolt out, loop the end of the drive wire around the pulley wheel and replace the bolt. The wires had to be under tension to work of course, but this could be relaxed to facilitate the strike manoeuvre by mounting the drive winches at the sides on steel plates with slots and lock nuts.

So, to dismantle, the lock nuts were loosened, the winch lifted and locked again to give slack. The hauling wire could be released from the return pulley and, once freed, the wire loop and 'skate' could be hauled out of the track and away from the diverter pulleys to be coiled up and tied to the frame of the support pier – no threading, no wire rope grips. The panels containing the tracks and forming the floor of the bridge were made to drop onto slightly conical bosses, also obviating the need for spanners.

These ideas had nothing to do with either the appearance of the moving 'stones' or their performance function. But with them we were able to reduce the pressure on the overworked crew and it was tacitly admitted that they had got the strike down to less than two hours. The cost of pre-erecting and extra thinking time at Sadlers Wells was well worth it.

The two masters had been served – the dynamic of the play and the need to ease the work load.

Lighting by Numbers . . .

Some years ago, a repertory theatre was producing *She Stoops to Conquer*. About two days or so before the fit-up weekend, there was a serious fire in the workshop premises, which were separate from the theatre. The damage was significant and a large amount of the scenery already prepared for the production was lost.

It was decided to go into hurry mode and recreate as far as possible what the designer had intended. This of course meant that the fit-up commenced with only those items of scenery which had been completed or could be quickly prepared. It also meant that during the course of the fit-up, unpainted pieces of scenery would appear on the set and subsequently, during periods when the company weren't rehearsing etc., the painters would continue decorating.

From a lighting point of view, which was my role, this made life very difficult because the stage was significantly brighter than was intended and as the production proceeded, the lighting states had to be consistently altered because the picture on the stage was changing all the time, which took even more time.

Is there a moral to this? Surely, the moral must be to investigate the practicality and cost of consequential loss insurance over and above cover for fire damage. In this way, at least the additional labour required to complete the scenery on time would have been recouped and/or the production could have been delayed by a few days. The insurance could have covered the reimbursement of the ticket holders for the cancelled performances.

A Slot In Time . . .
(or Maximise, Maximise, Maximise)

There once was a touring production of a well-known American musical. This production was specifically designed to tour and because of the size and complexity of the installation, it was decided to allow for a Tuesday opening, thereby denying the management of takings from a Monday night performance, equal to 12.5% of the total potential revenue. However, after a period of time on the tour, it became apparent that all the work was being completed before lunch on Tuesday and that the Tuesday afternoon time slot was basically going begging.

Subsequent to the tour, a discussion with the management raised the notion that had the production been made slightly simpler (and only slightly simpler) it would have been possible to open on the Monday night and gain the additional revenue (12.5%) or equally, the production could have been made significantly more complex and, perhaps, more attractive, at no great extra cost. Thus the management had fallen between two stools. The reason has to be submitted that this was because there was no imaginative Production Manager with an overview of the whole situation when the package was being put together.

The World Of Shakespeare / An Elizabethan Pageant

This 1980 Stratford-upon-Avon production brought a new facet of Production Management – the performance had no live performers! It was an 'audio visual' experience to be installed into a newly-built auditorium with a projected running time of 20-22 minutes. The audience stand in a space with a wide 'shelf' running all the way round at roughly head height. On this and running up to the ceiling are a series of tableaux populated with life size figures. If contemplated today, you would be looking for about £6m to complete it. This was a truly commercial venture. The contract between the supplier of the show (my employer) and the prospective owner/operator laid out strict deadlines for the each phase of the project. Architects, builders and others were all locked into the same series of time slots. At first I wondered at the rigidity, but I came to realise that spreading the pressure worked well. The phases bore onto the working arrangement between the supplier and the owner providing a series of steps whereby certain aspects could be agreed and then used as the basis of building the next step and so on. So when the designs were presented the client had an 'approval window', at the end of which they had to sign the design documents. In this way any additional requests from the owner could attract a further charge! Even such things as the day when the carpets would be laid were set over a year in advance. I could not plan any 'wet work' after that.

The production was intended for an extensive shelf life. Quality components were to be used throughout, without compromise. It's probably worth saying now that when the job was handed over I was provided with a folder of manuals in the event of equipment failure. Of course a maintenance manual had been supplied along with the 'show', but I had circuit diagrams and 'as builts' as well. I have not received a single call from the operators with any operational problems in over 20 years. During that time thousands of repeat performances have run. Using high quality equipment, especially for sound and lighting, and not stressing it to its limits, has paid enormous dividends.

My American employers, White Oak Design Inc. had done a number of similar presentations in the US. I went over to see some examples and familiarise myself with their office systems and routines. There were some surprises. For instance they had experienced difficulties in acquiring fibreglass materials which I kept assuring them were over-the-shelf items in the UK. They had had real problems with their static figures because of this. It was only after we got into the process here of positioning the figures at the end of an afternoon and leaving them to set over night that the fears were eventually laid to rest. A pleasant surprise was their post work watering hole called Victoria Station in Boston which was full of British railway memorabilia.

The whole process was to take the best part of 18 months and all of them were busy. On such a linear project you do not experience anything twice; it needs to be got right the first time. Company policy allowed time for extensive mullings before decisions were taken. When things were decided they usually had the agreement of all key parties so there was a feel of corporate responsibility which of course benefits working relationships. The work gave rise to many new experiences some more serious than others.

The figures needed to look as life-like as possible. I was told that the best way to start this was to take pictures of the proposed groups using real humans

The World of Shakespeare: the People Wall. This is used in the early section of the sequence. The models represent the different strata of contemporary society. Each one can be separately lit and there is a sky cloth behind. It started as a series of ply wood panels and the decorations were applied in successive layers. The Emblem in the middle was a real labour of love, involving many hours of craftsmanship. When complete it was extremely heavy and took several people pulling on a triple purchase block to haul it into position.

– us. This way we could shuffle about until the composition worked and then take the picture. The designer would then produce the costume drawings in the positions the characters were going to be in. We wanted a black background so the figures would stand out. I somehow knew that the Roundhouse had a black setting and arranged to spend the afternoon there on a non-matinee day. I bought some white tights and leotards and the office and production staff were volunteered for the modelling. The photos taken that afternoon, each carefully noting to which of the 70+ figures they related also became the design for the team making the figures. The air of mirth was just about concealed as we all pranced about in ill-fitting tight white kit! (The current owner of these odd images is unknown and probably doesn't realise the potential value of the trove.)

I found it odd that they hadn't closed off the top of the central space in the US examples I'd seen which seemed to create masking problems. We decided to put a ceiling in at Stratford which provided access above in the fit-up and holes could be cut where you needed to shine a light through. It also provided an excellent fix point for the leading edges of the scenery.

Lighting too had to be designed well in advance so that the building contractor could be made responsible for installing the bars and mounting points. Six months elapsed between doing the rig plan and the fit up. One had to constantly remind oneself that figures don't move. Therefore you don't have to put lights where people aren't going to go. There were also some low voltage units in the plot which made me worry about hum noise. I decided to dedicate one of the dimmer racks to low voltage and drop the voltage before the dimming took place. This meant that the LV units were being activated by 24V straight from the dimmer and that the transforming was done in a closed space well away from the auditorium.

There were points in the process where hard decisions had to be made. For instance, there were two dimmer manufacturers rather ahead of the others at the time. We had a policy of insisting that manufacturers install their own equipment, however, neither of the two big name dimmer makers wanted to install, preferring to send instructions to the onsite electrical contractor. We found another maker who would install, and modify his racks to our special needs without significant added costs. They were given the job and did it extremely well. Considering that the contract was for 120 channels (more than many theatres at the time) the attitude of certain big manufacturers still makes me shake my head.

Another choice was the all important control system. It had to be on a turnkey operable by FOH staff. We were still in the days of analogue dimmers and some very high figures were being bandied about for bespoke digital analogue conversion. In the end it boiled down to either a home-grown system which would encode the lighting cue information on the tape, automatically keeping it in synch with the sound track, or an American manufactured computer designed for running the services in office buildings but produced by a theatre lighting company. The decision criteria, price not being a big factor, went along the lines of . . . "UK kit close to base and back up, but somewhat limited it seemed to me in programming flexibility" . . . or . . . "US kit far from home, triggered by 10th second pulses with potential of making changes to the plot at any point at any time, probable back up delay, but, the programming team had used it before, so no familiarisation period would be needed (important on a fixed term contract)!

I wanted to go with the American system, but to do so we needed to do some fancy electronics linking the sound tape, the computer control and the key switch which set the whole show on the road. A lot of time was spent designing how we wanted this to happen. It ended like this: turning the key started the 8 track tape, one of the tracks carried the time pulses, as it moved forward the computer recognised the pulse signal and sent its first messages to the dimmer system, and so to the end where the tape deck instructed itself to stop and wind back. Once rewound it wound forward again at play speed to a magnetic cue stop and waited for the key to be turned again.

The physical installation in the space was contemporary with the final mixing of the sound tape. Many hours of effects, music, and spoken words had been recorded and had to be mixed onto the show tape. As noted above, one of the eight tracks carried the time pulse, the other seven carried separate signals to seven enormous speakers, six facing the audience and the seventh suspended above them. Halfway through the eight-week get in we had to clear up so the carpets could be laid. We were then able to test the speakers and start trial runs of the mixed tape. The mix had been done in a specially rigged studio with seven speakers replicating the positions of the full-size ones in the real space. The volumes were thus 'locked in' to a degree, but we programmed a re-visit after the first full space trials.

I invited several officers from the Warwickshire County Fire Brigade to the office we had rented in London to look at the model several months before the get-in. We discussed and agreed things like materials. I explained I wanted for speed of installation to erect a series of steel armature frames onto which painted and decorated panels could be hung. It also spread the contracts out so that I could seek competitive bids from scenic contractors to provide the decorative cladding for the separate steel frames. The frames would also give stable platforms for the set dressers to work on. This also considerably reduced the amount of potentially flammable softwood in the space. The fire risk was being minimised.

The required wiring code was another matter. The hard wired socket outlets for the lighting would be part of the builder's contract if the locations could be fixed before the performance space was handed over. If they had to be fixed to the setting then they would have to be made by us. A realistic view was taken, given that the performance platform was devoid of people other than maintenance staff, and the care we were taking to reduce flammability. We did have to do some hard wiring but we were allowed to use flex across the 'roof' to feed the lanterns aimed through holes and in the steel framed structures.

The World of Shakespeare: the Market Place. One end of the space was largely given over to the market. The life size figures are clustered in groups, each one of which related to part of the sound track. The sky was lit by some of the first CCT Minuette Fresnels to be made. The buildings are steel frames clad with ply panels.

A lot of potential work had been saved which more than compensated for the price of the lunch the fire officers enjoyed at a good Italian restaurant.

Painstaking though it may have appeared, we recorded and transcribed the regular meetings we had with contractors and suppliers and circulated the verbatim scripts to all concerned. Nothing was said about these. They would just arrive on people's desks. The effect was that meetings became very matter of fact with participants being much more precise about their work and its progress.

Small details were noted. We even went as far as to buy 'D' connectors for the ribbon cables in the control room and give one end to one contractor and the other to another and include the dedication for the conductors in the minutes. The outcome as far as control was concerned was that it took just over three days to install the computer from Ithaca Theatre Lighting and prove it operated the dimmers. The engineer from New York then had time on his hands but seemed quite unimpressed by the heady Shakespearean surroundings of Warwickshire in a cold February.

The path of true love does not run smooth as they say and so it proved for us at the start of the fit up. We encountered some of the severest winter weather for years and those parts of the building outside our performance space were barely started when we began. This meant loading in across the frozen mud of a building site and even using the adjacent public loo facilities – and of course there was no where to put anything. One of the scenic contractors had run into monumental cash flow problems on other jobs and our work had fallen behind. We had to terminate the agreement and collected all the unfinished work from his premises. We then employed some of his people to come and finish the work under our management in 'our' premises.

As we approached the opening and the show sequence was being run and tweaked we experienced random computer shut down problems. Vagaries in the electrical supply were suspected. The cause of the suspicion was of course the Royal Shakespeare Theatre just down the road. We tried unsuccessfully to relate the times of our problem to surges at the start of performances. A sensitive recording device showed several big spikes in the supply in a 24 hr period but none more than .2sec. A call to the US confirmed that the computer was protecting itself but was also being very cautious. We were allowed to instruct it to ignore any spike of .3sec or less. And thus it carried on happily for the next 20 years or so.

The experience was an important one for me. Everybody from the day of their first involvement knew that we were working to very strict time criteria. We also knew that quality work was expected throughout. Because it was never mentioned, getting 'behind was never a consideration. After 18 months, late on the afternoon of the day long set for hand over, we had our opening party and then handed over the keys to the running staff we had trained. It was years before I went back and nothing had changed. The benefits of strong management and sequential planning can never have been better exemplified. By the way we were on budget as well.

The Best or Worst of The Peter Principle

Some years ago as I was starting a new project I found myself staying in digs in the Midlands. In the same digs were two Austrian men who were in England to hand over one of those incredibly complicated looking yellow machines which align railway tracks you see skulking in the sidings . They admitted to being more than put out because the men they were training to operate the machines were in their sixties. The men, nearing retirement, had risen over many years to senior jobs in the track maintenance department of British Rail. Most of their lives and their training suited them for the manual work using a long wide tined fork. They were finding it difficult to get to grips with the high technology of the sophisticated machine. My lodging companions told me that almost anywhere else in the world they were handing over to much younger people who had engineering or technical qualifications and were competent to train future operators.

The result of the British Rail policy of automatic promotion was very expensive. Firstly the hand-over period had to be extended which entailed extra cost at the outset. Secondly, because of the men's age they would only be doing the job for a year or two before retiring. So, because their successors would be drawn from the same mould the manufacturers would have to send my colleagues back again, at more expense, to teach another pair of sexagenarians. Costs were being incurred for no gain. The theatre can rarely afford this luxury.

Back to Methuselah

This 1969 National Theatre production of *Back to Methuselah* was one of, if not the first, to be designed in England using the metric scale. The designer, Ralph Koltai, very sensibly decided to make it in 1:20 scale. Sensible because it was sufficiently larger than the 1:24 models that we were used to – to avoid confusion. 1:20 is a really easy scale to work with any metric ruler. The stage was to be surrounded with walls of clear Perspex 20" high. The ones at the sides had to be angled at the base to compensate for the raked stage 1:16.

ICI made Perspex. The largest sheet any one could supply was 10'x6'. However we were assured that half joints could be machined and when glued together would be as strong as the sheets themselves. Flame retardant Perspex, we found out , had a number of unhelpful qualities. It reacted very positively to humidity and temperature i.e. in cold dry conditions it would snap without warning. ICI told us that a 6" deflection over 20' would be the limit of tolerance. It also has a high coefficient of linear expansion.

Two issues needed to be addressed. Firstly, how to mount it and allow for the expansion factor. Consider here that under performance lighting it would have been fairly warm and would cool over night. Secondly, as it was to be in repertoire we needed a system for raising and lowering without bending. ICI also said that 20' had never been hung before and they expected a waisting effect.

Project: 20ft high Perspex wall 36ft wide, to be integrated into repertoire working.

Interestingly enough, we already had, *As You Like It*, designed by Ralph Koltai in the repertoire. Although I had not been involved specifically in the 'production' of *As You Like It*, I had taken the production on tour both into Europe, as far as Belgrade, and around the UK.

In this piece there were some panels consisting of steel frames and a clear plastic called Oroglas. There were also some Perspex tubes which hung down like long, tubular bells. Before I took it over for touring, the Oroglas had already developed a reputation for being extremely fragile. It was easy to note that the cracks frequently happened around the holes for the self-tapping screws which held the Oroglas on to the steel frames. If the flame-retardant Perspex had similar characteristics, then clearly we could not begin to consider anything which resembled any kind of bolt as a means of fixing. The Perspex tubes had also provided a stunning demonstration of just how dangerous the material could be. On tour, at Teatro La Fenice in Venice, during the fit-up, a flying bar containing several tubes managed to get in the way of an already suspended item as it was being flown out. This had the effect of putting downward pressure on one of the tubes. The tube detached itself and came down vertically. As it hit the floor, it shattered, as though it were a stream of cold water hitting a sink. The small pieces of plastic sprayed in all directions. It was quite frightening.

So, with these caveats in mind, we had to proceed fairly slowly. Having had reassurances from ICI that the material, when contact glued together, would be the same as if it were one piece, we eventually came up with the idea of gluing two additional thicknesses of the Perspex either side at the top, to create a kind of sandwich. We could then make a steel frame which, effectively, was a slot into which this sandwich could sit, so that the weight was held by two additional pieces glued either side. This also meant that there was no bolt fixing whatsoever and allowed the plastic to expand and contract at will within the "track" that we had provided at the top. We then decided that the best thing to do at the bottom would be to actually dead the pieces just above the stage floor, so that they would be hanging free and simply held in place by two pieces of angled section fixed down to the stage floor, which would prevent the wall, when in the vertical position, from swinging up or downstage.

There was a considerable conversation about the wisdom of handling the wall all at once or in single segments. Certainly this was going to be very heavy. It was calculated that three of the counterweight flying bars at the Old Vic would have adequate counter-weighting to lift the six sheets of the back wall, giving a total wall size of 20' high x 36' wide. My worry, as an ex-stage hand, was that getting six pieces vertical individually and then somehow attaching them to something existing, 20' up in the air, was a little too 'iffy'; although I did realise that the potential for disaster in raising this huge wall of plastic was very high indeed, given what ICI had said about deflections. We ended up realising that if each panel had its own steel mounting slot at the top, then the slot could be applied to the panel, the panel taken to the position for flying where a further steel sub-frame could exist underneath the clustered flying bars, with fixed suspension points. This, then, meant that as the panels were addressed, they could each be bolted securely in such a way that they would not bang into each other.

So far, so good. The next problem was the concern about deflection. We decided to make a series of wooden frames which, using timber 'on edge', held the plastic top and bottom and if one picked up one end, there would be no more than about 3" deflection over the whole length of 20'. These in fact became a very useful means of moving Perspex sheets around during changeovers and when they needed to be stored, so that the Perspex sheets were only 'on their own' when they were suspended in performance conditions on the stage. Thus, during the fit-up or strike, the wooden frame was attached by holding it up behind the sheet, hooking it on at the top, trapping it at the bottom and then each one had to be individually handled as the flying system lowered or raised the entire wall.

Next, we had the walls at the side to consider. At the time, The Old Vic had a rake of 1:16, so that each one of the panels had to be chamfered at the bottom to accommodate this. Not only that, they were completely non-interchangeable because the panels were grooved on the surface, thus the left and the right could not be similar. This proved to be one of the most worrying aspects of this production because, although we wanted to keep spare panels, the ones on the rear wall were interchangeable, but the ones on the side wall as noted here, were not. The expense of keeping six spares for the side walls was something we could not countenance and we had to resolve to take extra special care of these by giving them even more protection. In this case, the

Back to Methuselah: translucent Perspex spheres hang in space inside the clear Perspex walls. They reflect and reflections aid the impression of infinity.

wooden frames were made to be interchangeable and usable on either side of the stage by the bottom rail being pivotable to accommodate for the rake going in either direction. A similar system was used for raising and lowering each side, but of course they could not both be done at the same time. The afternoon when for the first time a wall of clear polished Perspex, 36' wide and 20' high, slowly rose from the stage floor to vertical was not without tension – but the result was stunning.

Once we had got the idea that Perspex should not be tight fixed a lot of other pieces of it in the show became easier to resolve. The eclipse disc seen in the illustration had two layers of plywood far enough apart for the Perspex to slide in. Holes went through the plywood. A larger hole went through the Perspex in which sat a good thick slice of old fashioned lab tubing. The bolt

Back to Methuselah: a time lapse photograph of the sweep of light reflecting off the 'Earth' which was set at the edge of the revolve, spinning through the spheres.

through the middle just moved about inside its rubber sleeve as the Perspex expanded and contracted.

This was an extraordinary learning curve. This whole procedure took several weeks of very careful investigation and exploration. We visited the ICI factory and learned a lot more about the plastic. The Licensing Authority took some interest, saying you can only have so many square feet of Perspex, etc. – but didn't know if this referred to both sides or not! Undeterred, we pressed on.

Back to Methuselah: a close up of the elipse disc. The Perspex rim is covered in layers of black flock, becoming more translucent towards the edge. The light sources (low voltage beam lights) were hung just upstage on a separate bar.

The play consists of five long acts and was being presented across two evenings. Many of the props and accessories were also in clear or white plastic and each one had to be individually specified. But amongst all the high tech modernity we had recourse to one of the oldest tricks in the book.

The opening sequence began with a gauze covering the entire opening of the stage. Projected images were to play on it before bleeding through and revealing the scenes in the pictures. But . . . a few years before the Old Vic had extended its stage well downstage of the original proscenium. There were several names for this hybrid forestage but there was no hiding the fact that

Back to Methuselah: the eclipse and the planets disappear. The solid 'earth'
sphere stops downstage centre before moving to the centre where it stops again,
this time in the centre of a little arbour made of clear perspex and green appliqué.
It then revolves again. The gap into which the sphere had to fit is clearly visible.
There were no margins for error. The 'earth' was drawn upstage on polished
perspex skids via a wire going to a winch. The friction in the skids obviated the
need for any kind of braking system and means of working it.

there was no real height above it and no grid. A 39' tumble pole was the answer. It was made partially in aluminium and the control lines at each end went to a motorised winch in the void space above. Provided even tension is maintained when applying the gauze to the pole it is a foolproof system; and so it was. Perhaps it was fitting for a play about timelessness that the oldest and the newest technologies were both being used at the same time.

Back to Methuselah is really five separate one-act plays. It begins with the Creation and goes as far into the future as one can imagine. When first opened it was played over two evenings, plays 1 – 3 on day one and 4 and 5 on day two. Play 4 always seemed very obscure and so it wasn't the biggest surprise to hear that 1, 2, 3 and 5 were to be given as one evening. In order for it not to take too long, one of the old interval changes was to become a quick scene change! This had never been in the designer's remit and the sets as they were, were hardly suitable.

The pictures here show Play 1, *The Garden of Eden*. Set on green felt, all that had to go at the end was the earth on its pole and the tree halo which flew out. Plays 3 and 5 both had revolving electrical complications so from Play 1 to Play 2 became the obvious quick change.

Play 2, almost conventional, consisted of a boarded floor outlining a room with carpets and 1920s furniture. The floor was square, but set on its long axis with one of the points downstage and below the revolve. The question was how fast could we set Play 2.

Setting furniture etc. was not a problem – there were plenty of people; the only issue was the floor. Clearly the existing heavy pieces would not work. For good design reasons a cloth would certainly not do. Ideas such as rolls of slats were looked at and eventually rejected.

Two or three years previously I had been talking to John Bury at Stratford. The RSC had been using a light-weight floor which was effectively a polystyrene sandwich: a layer of ply on the bottom stopped it fraying and the acrylic sheet on the top provided the decorative surface. This seemed the way forward – we could have thickness and lightness. The size was still a consideration because of the number of individual pieces which would need to be laid.

A truss spanned the Old Vic Stage, mid-stage or thereabouts, which left a gap of over 1ft (old measure) between the counterweight bars. This space seemed ideal for a thick item like a floor. Discussions ensued about the reliability of electric hoists as well as their consistency of performance. It was agreed to buy two chain hoists with consecutive serial numbers and wire them to the same contactor so their starts and stops would be synchronised. The floor would be flown into the big gap and lowered for use. Using motorised hoists removed the problem of weights needing to be unloaded. For mounting, we had V-shaped brackets made up which straddled the truss and bolted over the top and which were to be hauled up on a rope, so no access to the underside of the grid would be necessary. The chain would be unshackled at stage level and reversed back out of the way.

The floor itself had now become a dynamic object moving through 90°. I decided to have an aluminium chassis made with a hinge on the cross-stage diagonal. This would allow someone to grab the downward hanging point and guide it to its downstage mark, letting the rest follow, so to speak.

The 'chassis' was about 75mm thick and described the edge with lateral bracing. After being made it went to a second contractor who pop-riveted 2mm ply on to the bottom, filled the frame with dense expanded polystyrene and compressed it with a thicker pop-riveted layer of ply on the top. In this state it arrived at the National Theatre paint frame. Here, strips were laid on top simulating floor boards before painting and as a final touch the carpets were fixed down so the frilled edges remained free.

It looked a bit odd dangling up there, but it certainly worked. The scene change was well within the time allowed without being hurried – the crew enjoyed their new toy and probably didn't realise that we were one of, if not the first people to use chain hoists as part of the operation of a show – 33 years ago.

Necessity is the mother of invention.

"They're working on it"

When I took over technical responsibility for new productions at the National Theatre, I found myself in fairly regular contact with the Director. On one of the first occasions we met, he told me that he did not want to hear me say "they are working on it".

The previous incumbent of my responsibilities had been known to use this phrase on occasion. Clearly, as far as Sir Laurence was concerned, the evidence was that the repetition of the phrase was not frequently enough succeeded by the realisation of whatever it was that was supposed to be being worked upon.

Thus chastened, I developed a wider range of phrases, such as "something's being done about it", or, more obliquely, "they've started", but in the long run I realised that what our Director wanted was the truth. What he really quite reasonably expected from his Production Manager was a comprehensive, updated, situation report on every aspect of the incoming production's scenery and equipment whenever he enquired.

This led me in later years to be more inquiring when asking different departments as to their state of readiness. No longer was I prepared to take "we'll be another five minutes" from the lighting department. What I required to know was what had yet to be done, so that I could make my own judgement as to a realistic completion time. I believe it is absolutely essential, from the time when people begin training and throughout their careers, to encourage the culture of straightforwardness.

In Spain the Orientation Is Different

In Spain, with a touring production of *Macbeth*, we played the Corral dos Comedios at Almagro. This closely resembles a British Elizabethan inn-yard, rectangular in shape, with a stage at the far end and some seats on the level floor area in front of the stage. The building was open to the air.

The tour took place in high summer. Almagro is about 150 km south of Madrid, in the great open plain of La Mancha. The weather was unbelievably hot and the advertised performance time was 11 pm – presumably because by that time the searing heat had eased to a point where people would feel happy enough to sit in the open air. We decided to do most of our fit-up work at night and of course we had to light at night because of the necessity for darkness.

During one of the night work sessions, I remember having had to go down and spend some time resolving a few problems in the power supply and dimmer area, which was tucked underneath the stage. Having spent some time down there, I returned to the auditorium. As I walked in, a blast of hot, enervating air hit me and my immediate thought was "Oh, gosh, it's hot in here". But of course I was wrong, because I wasn't 'in' anywhere – I was 'out'!

Moral: try to remember where you are.

Spots Before Your Eyes

The designer's model showed a number of sticks coming out of the floor. At the top, they were angled, not unlike an ice hockey stick. They were green with yellow spots. Exploratory conversation revealed the fact that the designer would quite like it if the yellow spots could be seen as lights which were able to be controlled.

Whilst strolling down the road at dusk, with nothing particular (a common feature) in the mind, I noticed one of those all too common holes in the roadway. There was, by means of notice and protection, a kind of rope of lights. As I got closer, I became aware that the lights were inside a plastic tube. Instantly making the link between the designer's intentions and what I saw, I found pen and paper and, somewhere on the rope of lights, the name and telephone number of the manufacturers.

This led me to an extraordinary gentleman in Cornwall who had patented a flexible lamp-holder. Strings of these could be pulled through tubes. This delightful chap had had the good sense to show his invention to a significant digger of holes in roads, who had immediately ordered over 1m ft of the device. This caused the chap such stress that he had to give up his day job and devote his entire life to making strings of flexible lamp-holders. Although he had had nothing to do with the theatre before, he was happy to help and the result was satisfactory by everyone's agreement.

Moral: always take your reading glasses with you when you go for a walk.

Faithful Reproduction

There are a number of apocryphal tales of scenic artists faithfully reproducing the stain left by the coffee cup on the designer's artwork for the backcloth. There are so many, it must be supposed that more than one of them must to a degree be true.

This does mask the stronger reality. There was once a designer who finished off his model of a wooden fence in a Hungarian village by flicking ink from his fountain-type drawing pen on to the balsa wood planks. In scale, it looked weathered which, I am sure, is what the designer wanted. In the hands of an inexperienced scenic artist, the droplets of paint, faithfully reproduced, resembled something out of a Disney cartoon with Goofy about to appear: sixteen painted, beautiful drops, with round soft underparts and delicately fluted points at the top! Not at all what was wanted. Obviously, this was a retrievable situation, but at the same time it reminds Production Managers that there does need to be a discussion about the degree of faithfulness to which the model should be reproduced.

INDEX

ENTERTAINMENT TECHNOLOGY PRESS

FREE SUBSCRIPTION SERVICE

Keeping Up To Date with

Production Management

Entertainment Technology Press titles are continually up-dated, and all changes and additions are listed in date order in the relevant dedicated area of the publisher's website. Simply go to the front page of www.etnow.com and click on the BOOKS button. From there you can locate the title and be connected through to the latest information and services related to the publication.

The author of Production Management can be contacted via the publishers email at editor@etnow.com.